THE LIBRARY OF HISTORY AND DOCTRINE

DID THE EARLY CHURCH
BAPTIZE INFANTS?

THE LIBRARY OF HISTORY AND DOCTRINE

The aim of this international Library is to enable scholars to answer questions about the development of the Christian tradition which are important for an understanding of Christianity today

Editorial Cummittee

S. L. GREENSLADE, Regius Professor of Ecclesiastical History, Oxford (*Chairman*)

HENRY CHADWICK, Regius Professor of Divinity, Oxford

OWEN CHADWICK, Dixie Professor of Ecclesiastical History, Cambridge

G. W. H. LAMPE, Ely Professor of Divinity, Cambridge

JOHN T. McNEILL, Auburn Professor Emeritus of Church History, Union Theological Seminary, New York

E. GORDON RUPP, Professor of Ecclesiastical History, Manchester

T. F. TORRANCE, Professor of Christian Dogmatics, Edinburgh

BV813.2
A413

DID THE EARLY CHURCH BAPTIZE INFANTS?

KURT ALAND
Professor in the University of Münster

Translated with an Introduction by
G. R. BEASLEY-MURRAY
Principal of Spurgeon's College, London

and with a Preface by
JOHN FREDERICK JANSEN
Austin, Texas

Philadelphia
The Westminster Press

132036

JUL 1 1969

Copyright © SCM Press Ltd. 1963

Translated by G. R. Beasley-Murray from the German
*Die Säuglingstaufe im Neuen Testament und in der Alten Kirche:
Eine Antwort an Joachim Jeremias*
Chr. Kaiser Verlag, München, 1961

Library of Congress Catalog Card No. : 63-8863

PRINTED IN GREAT BRITAIN

To
The Society of Biblical Literature and Exegesis
in warm appreciation
of my election as honorary member

CONTENTS

ABBREVIATIONS

Arndt and Gingrich	W. F. Arndt and F. W. Gingrich, *Greek-English Lexicon of the New Testament* (being an ET of W. Bauer, *Griechisch-Deutsches Wörterbuch*[4], 1952), Cambridge, 1957.
CC	Corpus Christianorum, Turnhout, 1953 ff.
CIG	*Corpus Inscriptionum Graecarum.*
CSEL	Corpus Scriptorum Ecclesiasticorum Latinorum, Vienna.
ET	English translation.
GCS	Die Griechischen Christlichen Schriftsteller der ersten drei Jahrhunderte, Leipzig and Berlin.
HE	*Historia ecclesiastica.*
JTS	*Journal of Theological Studies*, Oxford.
Kraft	H. Kraft, *Texte zur Geschichte der Taufe, besonders der Kindertaufe in der alten Kirche* (Kleine Texte 174), Berlin, 1953.
MPG	Migne, *Patrologia Graeca*, Paris
MPL	Migne, *Patrologia Latina*, Paris
RGG	*Die Religion in Geschichte und Gegenwart*, Tübingen.
TU	Texte und Untersuchungen, Leipzig and Berlin.
WA	Weimar edition of Luther's works.
ZNW	*Zeitschrift für die neutestamentliche Wissenschaft*, Berlin.

AUTHOR'S PREFACE TO THE
ENGLISH EDITION

THIS STUDY arose from a request for a contribution to a volume in celebration of the ninetieth birthday of Erich Klostermann on 14 February
1960. The investigation had to correspond to the area of work of the one in
whose honour it was produced, and that included the New Testament and
the early period of Church History. Of possibilities that fell to be considered, the question of infant baptism, vigorously discussed for decades,
appeared to be the most relevant and rewarding, both as a topic and by
reason of the issues bound up with it. The work was therefore commenced,
with little idea as to the results to which a study of the early history of
infant baptism would lead, and without undue concern as to whether they
would justify the expenditure and labour, although the problem had been
discussed from varied angles and in some voluminous contributions. From
these contributions and discussions it became plain that the group that
asserted with confidence the practice of infant baptism from the beginning
of the Church was increasingly dominating the scene. The work of
Joachim Jeremias, *Die Kindertaufe in den ersten vier Jahrhunderten*,[1]
appeared to make this position impregnable. It was expounded in brilliant
style; in it Jeremias utilized everything known to exist in the sources,[2] as
well as in more recent literature,[3] and he summarized all the arguments
that have been brought into play up to the present.

The result of the present author's labours was surprising, indeed dis-
maying. The more his work on the subject advanced, the greater became
his perplexity. He therefore subjected the results of his studies to the
exacting test of a seminar on infant baptism, to see whether they could be
maintained in discussion, and he submitted a preliminary draft of the
manuscript to two colleagues for their critical judgment. To his surprise

---

[1] Göttingen, 1958. The book has been translated into English by David Cairns under
the title *Infant Baptism in the First Four Centuries*, published by the SCM Press, 1960.
[2] Their enumeration comprises twelve pages of bibliography (six in the English
edition).
[3] The list of works takes up five pages (three in English).

and gratification they concurred with him and urged him to continue in this work. The result was the study *Die Säuglingstaufe im Neuen Testament und in der alten Kirche*, Munich, 1961; thanks to the kindly co-operation of the SCM Press it is now presented in an English edition. The initiative for this came from Principal Beasley-Murray, to whom I express my gratitude not only for this but also for the labour of translating the book into English. He has been good enough to contribute an introduction, to orientate the English-speaking reader to the debate on infant baptism and the problems bound up with it.

This is the more important, in that my investigation is almost exclusively related to the argument of Joachim Jeremias, as it took final form in the volume *Infant Baptism in the First Four Centuries*.[1] This does not signify a depreciation of other works written from a similar viewpoint. The conversation with Jeremias is itself conducted on the basis of the sources, without making recourse to the literature which is opposed to his views. The position of Jeremias has been chosen for discussion because it is so extensively and thoroughly built up. By this means it has been possible to enter on a discussion concerning infant baptism conducted entirely on the basis of the sources. So far as they have been employed by Jeremias, they are examined to see whether the interpretation he draws from them is the only one possible or whether they ought to be interpreted in another manner. So far as they have not been used by him, they serve both to control and to construct yet further results gained by the first procedure. By this means the essentials are most easily appreciated and needless debates are avoided. The author is concerned to establish what can and what cannot be said about the existence and practice of infant baptism in the earliest times. The sources have to provide the answer; all else is of secondary import. Moreover the author—who from the beginning desires to make it clear that he regards the practice of infant baptism in the Church today as both needful and legitimate—is not of the opinion that his interpretation of the sources is in all respects the only one possible. Some of the texts are too complicated for such assurance. But he does consider that the result of his investigations, that infant baptism is certainly provable only from the third century and that its earliest literary traces belong to the outgoings of the second century, cannot be contested from the sources.

Münster, Westphalia   KURT ALAND
December 1961

---

[1] The English edition of this work, published in 1960, introduces certain changes as compared with the German original of 1958; naturally account has been taken of these changes in the present edition.

PREFACE FROM AMERICA

ALTHOUGH the question of infant baptism is certainly not new, it has assumed particular importance in recent theological discussions. The reasons for this vigorous and lively debate are not hard to find.

For one thing, an impatient concern for reality in worship and in life has made the Church acutely aware that far too often her baptismal practice has been a casual nod in the direction of a *Corpus Christianum* which has little basis in fact. Already in 1937, Emil Brunner protested that most of our contemporary neopagans had been baptized as infants. 'What does the fact of having been baptized mean for a large number of contemporary people who do not know and do not even care to know whether they have been baptized?'[1] Who is not aware that frequently infant baptism has been based more upon conformity than upon conviction?

Again, the ecumenical movement raises the whole question of baptism. After all, baptism is not only important in itself; it is also closely related to the unity of the Church. What is the nature of the unity we seek? Ecumenical conversation cannot divorce the doctrine of the Church from the doctrine of baptism, the sacrament of initiation into the Church. Happily our contemporary discussions are abandoning the older polemics when separate traditions shouted over each others' shoulders. We are learning a humbler and more brotherly spirit as our various traditions seek together to learn what 'one baptism' means. We are finding that Christian baptism is an essential element both in our unity and in our disunity as churches. As the conference at Oberlin put it: 'Of the churches which practise infant baptism we ask . . . What is the responsibility of the Church to the baptized person who does not become a believer?' Similarly, 'Of the churches which practise only believers' baptism, we ask: Is sufficient justice done among you to the fact that God's grace is active in and through the Christian community from the very beginning of a person's life, preparing him for the full confession and experience of the faith?'[2]

---

[1] E. Brunner, *The Divine-Human Encounter*, trans. A. W. Loos, London and Philadelphia, 1943, p. 181.
[2] *The Nature of the Unity We Seek :* Official Report of the North American Conference on Faith and Order, ed. Minear, St Louis, Bethany, 1958, p. 199.

Moreover, the revival of biblical theology has given new impetus to the study of baptism. Increased awareness of the cultic and confessional framework of the New Testament is contributing to a fresh interest in the worshipping life of the New Testament Church.

Finally, the liturgical renewal has prompted investigations not only in New Testament study but also in the history of early Christianity.

The disagreement regarding infant baptism has its ironies. For example, a Baptist theologian remarks that his own tradition has moved in practice, though not in theory, towards child baptism by urging the call to discipleship and baptism before the child reaches the years of adolescence. On the other hand, the most vigorous protests against infant baptism have come recently from within the Reformed tradition which practises infant baptism.

Especially in Europe the debate has had vigorous expression from the 1940's. For example, at Basel two distinguished colleagues have taken radically opposite views. Karl Barth, in his *The Teaching of the Church Regarding Baptism* (1948), has given the most serious challenge yet raised to infant baptism. Oscar Cullmann's reply, *Baptism in the New Testament* (1950), has had equal attention and wide influence. To these we could add a score of other important names.

However, the most exhaustive attempt to vindicate infant baptism on historical grounds is the able volume by Joachim Jeremias, *Infant Baptism in the First Four Centuries*. (Jeremias first published his work in 1938, but this English edition is a translation from the revised German edition of 1958.) His method is historical, for he is confident that the New Testament, the documents, and the inscriptions of the first centuries all give cumulative testimony to the practice of infant baptism. In the fourth century, on the other hand, he sees a temporary crisis for infant baptism, but one soon overcome by the ancient Church. Jeremias is a master of so marshalling evidence—even when some of it is ambiguous—that the impact of his book is one of very substantial demonstration. (Those who are acquainted with his *Eucharistic Words of Jesus* will recall the similar painstaking zeal with which he seeks to demonstrate that the Last Supper was indeed a Passover meal.)

And now, just when Jeremias seemed to have won the field on historical grounds, Kurt Aland has published his *Die Säuglingstaufe im Neuen Testament und in der alten Kirche* (1961). It is an answer to Jeremias through a point by point refutation of the latter's main contentions. In contrast to Jeremias, Aland insists that there is no direct witness for infant baptism before the third century, and that the data before and after this period argue for the novelty rather than the antiquity of the practice.

Readers will be grateful that this debate is now available in English, and that a translation of the reply by Professor Jeremias is being prepared, for it is not likely that historical research as such will be able to add very much to what the three volumes offer. This preface does not need to summarize findings nor to offer a value judgment. Instead, it invites the reader to study the case for himself and to weigh the relative strength of both positions. It is in order, however, to make some observations regarding the necessity and the limits of such historical investigation. Since baptism is based upon and witnesses to a history of salvation (*Heilsgeschichte*), it follows that historical investigation of its practice is legitimate and necessary. The task which Jeremias and Aland assay is an important one. They both realize its complexity. Research into the history of the Church's life and worship must try to work back from the known traditions of the ancient Church (in this case the third century), and it must try to work forward from the actual New Testament period. Because the data are fragmentary it would be wrong methodologically to say that elements from the second or third centuries not mentioned in the New Testament are necessarily non-existent then. At the same time, it would be erroneous to assume that later tradition is always a faithful and consistent continuation of the New Testament Church. Withal, the New Testament theologian knows that he must take history seriously. Thirty years ago, the authors of *The Riddle of the New Testament* put the matter in these words: 'The Christian religion is not merely open to historical investigation, but demands it, and its piety depends upon it. . . . Christian theology has been creative in the field of historical investigation because the theologian has been compelled to a delicate sense for the importance of history by a faith which is grounded upon a particular event.'[1]

At the same time, the present debate illustrates the fact that historical investigation into the origins of Christian faith has its limits—and this for two reasons. The actual data are sufficiently ambiguous for two competent scholars to be able to arrive at opposite verdicts about the same materials. Apart from this, however, there is a deeper reason why historical investigation has its limits in probing the meaning of faith. Hoskyns and Davey, in the work just mentioned, go on to say: 'The New Testament documents do, in fact, yield to the modern critical method; and yet the solution of the historical problem does nothing either to compel faith or to encourage unbelief. There are here no "assured results" of New Testament criticism.

[1] E. Hoskyns and N. Davey, *The Riddle of the New Testament*, London, 1931, p. 10.

The historian can help to clarify the issue, but no more. . . . Here, then, the historian is driven to lay down his pen, not because he is defeated; not because his material has proved incapable of historical treatment, but because, at this point, he is faced by the problem of theology. . . .'[1]

Indeed, the question of infant baptism is a problem of theology. It will not be settled finally by historical demonstration—even if more evidence is forthcoming. It will be settled by the meaning of baptism, for it is ultimately a doctrinal decision.

This is not said to minimize the importance of historical investigation but to underscore the character of faith. For example, historical research will continue to probe the origins of John's baptism—and the last few years have uncovered more data. None the less, a study of origins will not adequately interpret John's rite because, whatever its origins, it witnesses to a new reality. Similarly, we may and we must seek historical understanding of the relation between John's baptism and Christian baptism, and yet the latter will not be explained by the former because it bears witness to a new reality. Again, although the historian must weigh the evidence as to the probabilities about infant baptism in the earliest Church, the missionary situation of that early community was unique and unrepeatable. Therefore, whether infant baptism is a valid expression in the later Church depends not so much on whether this continuity can be externally demonstrated but on whether it is now a faithful witness to New Testament baptism.

Aland realizes this. Jeremias rests his case overmuch on historical demonstration as such—brilliant, painstaking, and persuasive as this may be. Aland, on the other hand, after offering his own hypothesis regarding the origin of infant baptism, concludes with an epilogue, 'Infant Baptism Today?' He rightly suggests that too often the case has been put in one of two alternatives: *Either* the New Testament Christians and the early Church practised infant baptism and therefore we should today, *or* there was no practice of infant baptism in the New Testament period and in the early Church and therefore only believers' baptism is legitimate today. But, he insists, one must rather say that the New Testament indicates the character and meaning of baptism without spelling out its manner of administration. Accordingly, theological fidelity more than methodological continuity will determine our decision. As a hymn puts it, 'New occasions teach new duties'.

To repeat, the decision regarding infant baptism ultimately must rest on doctrinal grounds. And yet, the doctrinal question cannot be raised

[1] *Ibid.*, pp. 179, 182.

abstractly. Always the Church is driven back to her beginnings and to her scriptures. That is what makes the present exchange between Jeremias and Aland such an exciting and rewarding experience. It epitomizes the problem of New Testament study. It is a humbling reminder that 'we know in part'. Above all, it asks us to re-examine our practice and to see again how baptism must focus and interpret the meaning of the new life in Christ.

The Austin Presbyterian   JOHN FREDERICK JANSEN
Theological Seminary
Austin, Texas

The Baptismal Controversy in the British Scene

CONTROVERSY on baptism is no more a novelty in Britain than on the Continent. As the Anabaptists engaged in public disputations with Zwingli in Zürich, so the later Baptists entered into verbal and literary debates with Anglicans and others in this country. The discussions evidently did not lack warmth, as the titles of the works that were issued indicate. Daniel Featley's *The Dipper Dipt* (1644) was answered by Henry Denne's *Antichrist Unmasked* (1645); Samuel Fisher's *Baby Baptism mere Babism* (1653) was matched by Richard Carpenter's *The Anabaptist washt and washt and shrunk in the washing* (1653). It is a relief to find that one John More could issue a work entitled, 'A lost ordinance restored; or eight questions in reference to the laying on of hands lovingly answered by one of the least of saints, with a general exhortation to all baptized Churches not yet under the practice' (1654). A more amicable spirit among the contestants gradually prevailed, but C. H. Spurgeon's sermon on baptismal regeneration, preached in June 1864, let loose a pamphlet war as violent as anything that has been seen in this country. Spurgeon believed that the views of the Tractarians raised the issue whether salvation was by baptism or the blood of Christ: 'Believe me, it is no trifle. It may be that on this ground Armageddon shall be fought. . . . Out of any system which teaches salvation by baptism must spring infidelity, an infidelity which the false Church already seems willing to nourish and foster beneath her wing. God save this favoured land from the brood of her own established religion!' Not unnaturally this language was repaid in kind and with interest. The Rev. Charles Wills issued a pamphlet entitled, *Rev. C. H. Spurgeon Settled*, bearing on the title page the legend, 'If thou hast not sense enough to speak, have wit enough to hold thy tongue, Popular Proverb'. This in turn called forth a reply, *Great is Diana, or, Mother Church and the Babes, a Rejoinder to the Rev. Charles Wills' playful tractate . . .*, by R. A. Bellman. Anglicanism was defended in a pamphlet, *Spurgeonism logically developed, A Few Suggestions adapted to Mr Spurgeon's 'Small Logical Faculty'* (a

B

reference to Spurgeon's admission that his logical faculty was limited), and a Baptist produced an essay with the prize title, *Regeneration or Degeneration, A Pill for the Parsons and a Spur for Spurgeon*, by Grandfather Ignatius. An abundance of tracts were issued in similar style. To what extent the churches were edified by this mutual vilification is doubtful.

Today gladiatorial combat in the arena has been replaced by discussion about a table, but while less blood is shed, it is extraordinarily easy for temperatures to rise when infant baptism is on the agenda. In part this is due to the extent to which we are bound up with the life of our churches; we are personally indebted to them beyond measure and we are correspondingly hurt when our own tradition is called in question. Yet the unleashing of emotion in ecclesiastical discussions is quite unreasonable, for every theologian is aware that his own tradition stands censured by some aspect of New Testament teaching and that none of the others is without some support from the foundation source. In this book the term 'presupposition' occurs frequently, though I have disguised it at times; there is no doubt that the presuppositions we bring to this study materially affect our view of contending positions in the debate. Here the author challenges a traditional and, till recently, a well nigh universally held presupposition, namely that infant baptism goes back to the primitive Church and was authorized by the Apostles. Now it demands much of members of the great churches to contemplate the negation of that conviction coldly; for is not the practice itself, and therefore the foundation of membership in the Church, thereby called in question? Many will unhesitatingly answer in the affirmative. An introductory statement to the first interim report of the Church of Scotland Commission on baptism appealed to the Presbyteries to consider the report carefully: 'In so doing the Commission would say, as did the writers of the Scots Confession of 1560, that if anyone can show from Holy Scripture that anything erroneous is contained herein, they promise them that they will either prove from Holy Scripture that the criticism is itself erroneous or amend what is amiss to bring it into conformity with the Word of God.'[1] That is a brave statement, but it is a dangerous one; it could only come from those who are very confident of their stand, and it also makes it difficult for those who assert it to face the kind of criticism which this book offers, for to admit the possibility that it may be right is all but unthinkable.

Now I doubt whether the majority of ministers and clergy in Britain

---

[1] The Church of Scotland, *Interim Report of the Special Commission on Baptism*, May 1955, p. 2.

realize to what extent their scholars in this century have repudiated the presupposition to which we refer and would be embarrassed by a statement such as that made by the Scottish divines. German Biblical scholarship has always been more radical than ours, but the fact that such writers as W. Heitmüller,[1] F. M. Rendtorff,[2] Paule Feine,[3] and Hans Windisch[4] in the opening decade of this century all declared that infant baptism was not a practice of the primitive Church could not but affect the theologians of this country. Accordingly we find that P. T. Forsyth in the following decade declared, 'There is no infant baptism in the New Testament. It is within the principle of the Gospel, but not in the New Testament use. It is so in every mission. And Christianity began as a mission.'[5] Forsyth incorporated in his book an essay by a fellow Congregationalist, H. T. Andrews, 'The Place of the Sacraments in the Teaching of St Paul'; the latter made the remark in passing, as though argument was unnecessary, 'There is no shred of real proof that baptism was ever administered to infants in the Apostolic Age'.[6]

The Presbyterian theologian H. R. Mackintosh, discussing objections to infant baptism, referred to that offered by the alleged absence of the practice from the New Testament: 'No answer is possible to the objection,' he said, 'except to admit it frankly.'[7] He cited the popular proofs to the contrary, namely the saying as to the holiness of children, I Cor. 7.14, our Lord's blessing of children, Mark 10.13 ff., and household baptisms in Acts: 'The passage dealing with mixed marriages in I Cor. 7.12 ff. plainly indicates that in the Apostolic Age it had not occurred to any of the religious leaders that children should be baptized, even when the father or mother was a Christian. . . . When (our Lord's) beautiful saying that to enter the Kingdom we need to become like little children is quoted in support of infant baptism, it is forgotten that the childlike mind He declares to be essential is not the absence of consciousness, but the presence of real trust, humility and wonder. . . . It is true that no cogent proof can be given that none of the Christian households or house fellowships of that date included very young children. It would certainly be odd if it were not so in some one case; only, even so the children may not have been

<hr />

[1] *Im Namen Jesu*, Göttingen, 1903, and *Taufe und Abendmahl im Urchristentum*, Tübingen, 1911.
[2] *Die Taufe im Urchristentum im Lichte der neueren Forschungen*, Leipzig, 1905.
[3] Art. 'Taufe: I, Schriftlehre', *Realencyklopädie für protestantische Theologie und Kirche*, 3rd ed., vol. 19, Leipzig, pp. 369 ff.
[4] *Taufe und Sünde im ältesten Christentum bis auf Origenes*, Tübingen, 1908.
[5] *Lectures on the Church and Sacraments*, London, 1917, p. 168.
[6] *Op. cit.*, p. 150.
[7] 'Thoughts on Infant Baptism', *The Expositor*, 8th ser., vol. xiii, 1917, p. 195.

baptized.'¹ The arguments have not greatly changed since Mackintosh's time, on the one side and the other!

Among Methodists of more recent times Robert Nelson may be regarded as typical: 'That the New Testament says nothing explicitly about the baptizing of little children is incontestable,' he wrote.² He cites the three proof texts for infant baptism dealt with by Mackintosh and dismisses them in similar fashion, adding that in current discussion greater weight must be placed on theological rather than scriptural grounds for infant baptism.

The most striking change of attitude to the New Testament teaching on baptism, however, is manifest in the Anglican communion. The views of its theologians and liturgiologists have hardly been moulded by Continental thinkers—the names of Barth and Brunner, Cullmann and Jeremias seldom occur in Anglican publications on baptism. I have the impression that one single consideration has dominated Anglican thinking on Baptism more than all others, namely the conviction that the *theology* of baptism in the New Testament presumes the recipients of the rite to be mature persons. One finds this as early as Charles Gore: 'The Christian rites were, of course, designed for adult converts. . . . All the early lore about baptism, and the early ritual emphasize the element of solemn and deliberate choice—the "dying to live". This situation continued on the whole for some three centuries. . . . "Baptism doth represent unto us our profession"—it is profession of discipleship. . . .'³ Gore did not believe that infant baptism was not practised in the primitive Church, and he certainly did not question its use today, apart from urging that its indiscriminate application has been 'the real disaster' of the Church.⁴ N. P. Williams expressed fundamentally similar views to these in his Bampton Lectures, but he went further than Gore: 'The New Testament references to initiation assume that its recipients are adults, and that the dispositions required in them are those of conscious and deliberate renunciation of sin and idols, and of personal faith and allegiance to Christ. Thus conceived, the rite illustrates vividly the true principles of ethical sacramentalism, which demand not merely the due performance of a sacred act by the minister but the right response of heart and will on the part of the worshipper.'⁵ Accordingly the attempt to attribute infant baptism to the Apostles is to be deprecated: 'That infants may and should be baptized is a proposition which rests solely upon the actual practice of the Church; as

---

¹ *Ibid.*   ² *The Realm of Redemption*, London, 1951, p. 129.
³ *The Reconstruction of Belief*, London, 1926, pp. 749–51.
⁴ *Op. cit.*, p. 750.
⁵ *Ideas of the Fall and of Original Sin*, London, 1927, p. 550.

in the fifth century the sole argument for the fact is simply this: "The Church does baptize infants, and we cannot suppose that the Church has acted wrongly or without good cause in so doing".[1] In this writer's view infant baptism arose neither from theological nor ecclesiastical motives; it was essentially a popular movement from below, springing from the sub-conscious instincts of the people; in the process it generated 'a not inconsiderable body of doctrinal ideas in order to effect its own *ex post facto* justification.'[2]

N. P. Williams was more radical than the majority of Anglican theologians, but others who have kept to a more central path have expressed kindred views. The most representative exposition of Anglican sacramental theology is O. C. Quick's *The Christian Sacraments*;[3] almost the entire discussion of baptism in his book is taken up with the difficulties caused by the change in the Church's practice of adult baptism as the normal mode of initiation to that of infant baptism.[4] This question has similarly actuated the provocative Gregory Dix in his search for a solution of the baptismal problem, although he adopted a different course from that of Quick. He considered that in treating infant baptism as the norm, and adult baptism as an occasional anomaly, the Prayer Book was under the sway of a mediaevalism that had abandoned the scriptural pattern.[5] Accordingly he laid down three principles for a right understanding of Christian Initiation: (i) baptism into the death and resurrection of Christ and the Pentecostal baptism of the Spirit are not one thing but two, both necessary and inseparable; (ii) salvation cannot be passively received, i.e. it is radically incomplete until the fullness of the new divine life from within the Christian has been bestowed; (iii) Christian initiation in the New Testament is thought of solely in terms of a *conscious* adherence and response to the Gospel of God, that is, solely in terms of adult initiation.[6] If, therefore infant baptism is to continue as the usual form of the rite (and Dix did not desire it otherwise), it must be viewed as 'always an abnormality, wholly incomplete by itself and absolutely needing completion by the gift of the Spirit and the conscious response of faith.'[7]

The reports issued in the post-war years by the Church of England's Joint Committees on Baptism, Confirmation and Holy Communion,[8] and the later one from the Liturgical Commission,[9] have proceeded on closely

---

[1] *Op. cit.*, p. 551. [2] *Op. cit.*, p. 221. [3] 2nd ed., London, 1932. [4] See pp. 168–80.
[5] *The Theology of Confirmation in Relation to Baptism*, London, 1946, p. 28.
[6] pp. 30–31. [7] p. 31.
[8] *Confirmation Today*, London, 1944; *The Theology of Christian Initiation*, 1948; *Baptism Today*, 1949; *Baptism and Confirmation Today*, 1955.
[9] *Baptism and Confirmation*, 1959.

parallel lines. Of these reports it would appear that the one issued in 1948, *The Theology of Christian Initiation*, represents the decisive determination of Anglican baptismal theology, and from it, in fact, those responsible for shaping the thought and practice of the Church of England have not deviated. Christian Initiation is viewed as an entry into the eternal world that in Christ broke into this one: 'The rites of initiation mark the passage of the convert into this new world. It is assumed in all the New Testament language about the rites that the convert receives them with a lively faith and a renunciation of the old world. And the rites bestow far more than admission to a society, for they are the focus of a creative action of God whereby a man is made one with Christ in his death and resurrection, cleansed from his sin, admitted into the fellowship of the Ecclesia which is Christ's Body, given the adoption of Sonship to the Father, and sealed with the Holy Spirit unto the day of redemption. . . . Our problem today is not just the doctrine and practice of baptism but the recovery of the primitive fullness of conception wherein Christian initiation has its meaning.'[1] It is further observed that the note of personal response is conspicuous in the New Testament rites: 'The great privileges bestowed in baptism are inseparable from the "hearing of faith" and the conscious renunciation of the pagan world.' It is therefore urged that the baptism of infants cannot bear this weight of theological meaning attributed to initiation in the New Testament; that requires the total complex of baptism, confirmation and first communion.[2] This position is further developed in the final report of the Committee, *Baptism and Confirmation Today*, and an adventurous endeavour is made to implement it in the experimental service book, *Baptism and Confirmation*, wherein the 'Ministration of Baptism and Confirmation to those who are of Age to Answer for Themselves' is set out as the archetypal baptismal service and the other orders of baptism are patterned on it. This represents perhaps the boldest step in theological and liturgical reform of any state Church since the Reformation, and its consequence cannot yet be foreseen.

A very different impression is gained from the study documents issued by the Church of Scotland's Commission on baptism.[3] As is to be expected, the emphasis in these documents falls on the theological implications of baptism, and there is much in their theological interpretation for which all the Churches must be grateful. Nevertheless a real weakness is evident in the treatment of the issue with which we are concerned, and in the

[1] p. 9.   [2] p. 12.
[3] *The Church of Scotland Interim Reports of the Special Commission on Baptism*, Edinburgh, 1955, 1956, 1957, 1958, 1959.

judgment of not a few it mars to no small degree the contribution of these reports. In contrast to the theologians of the Church of England, the Church of Scotland's theologians stand by the tradition of their forebears in regarding infant baptism as the normative pattern baptism. 'For them (the Scottish Reformers) baptism by its very nature as the sacrament of our first entrance into God's household was essentially relevant for children, but therefore equally adaptable to adults, who can only enter into the Kingdom of God as little children.'[1] Not surprisingly they adhere to 'the unanimous view of the Ancient Catholic Church' that regards infant baptism as 'the unchallenged practice of the Christian Church from the beginning'.[2] The idea of 'believers' baptism', exclusive of infants, is characterized as 'entirely modern'; it issues from 'the Renaissance idea of human individualism and autonomy' and represents 'a radical divergence from the Biblical teaching about the nature of man'.[3]

Naturally this entails a demonstration that infant baptism is to be found in the New Testament; the proof is provided by some extraordinary exegesis. Matt. 11.25 f. is cited to show that children have a unique place in the Kingdom; the passage is held to reflect Ps. 8, and the comment is added, 'It seems clear that the relation of little children to the Father is understood as mediated through the Sonship of Christ. Little children may not know what they are saying, but Jesus is Himself their cry to the Father.'[4] The reader should check the passage for himself and ask whether he thinks that is a just deduction from it; I may be pardoned for suggesting it to be irrelevant. Matt. 18.6 refers to 'little ones who believe in me'; it is suggested that this phrase either denotes little ones *baptized* to Christ (on the assumption that 'baptize into' = 'believe into'), or it relates to actual *belief* in Christ. If the latter is true, the report comments, it is 'a staggering thing to say of "little ones" '.[5] If the 'little ones' are infants it is undoubtedly staggering; but in that case we are to understand that 'Matthew wants us to see that the rational order is reversed in relation to Jesus Christ'.[6] The Blessing of the Children, Mark 10.13 ff. and parallels, is first viewed in the light of Cullmann's belief that κωλύειν (hinder) reflects a baptismal liturgical usage, hence the incident is intended by the Evangelists to serve as an authorization of infant baptism,[7] and the procedure of Jeremias is then followed in setting out Matt. 18.3, Mark 10.15, Luke 19.17 in parallelism with John 3.3 and 3.5 as all expressive of one idea, namely *new birth through baptism*.[8]

[1] *1958 Report*, p. 12. [2] *1955 Report*, p. 20.
[3] *Ibid.* In the 1956 *Draft Interim Report with Supporting Material*, believers' baptism is said to be 'essentially a modern phenomenon, first found in AD 1140'; the reference is to the Paulicians of Armenia. [4] *1955 Report*, p. 22. [5] p. 23. [6] *Ibid.* [7] p. 24. [8] p. 25.

Acts provides examples of household baptisms; the presumption that young children were included in the baptisms is believed to be strengthened by 'the Biblical way of speaking of households', i.e. as specifically including little children.[1] In the Epistles appeal is made to the fact that children (τέκνα) are addressed in Eph. 6.1 ff.; since the Letter is addressed to the 'saints and faithful in Christ Jesus' (1.1), children are evidently included among them and therefore must have been baptized—presumably as infants. In I John 2.12–14 the writer not only singles out little children (παιδία) but he also specifically addresses infants (τεκνία), who have been anointed with the chrism of the Spirit (2.28) and have been born of God (2.29); this, of course means (though the writers have not pointed it out) that these 'infants' are exhorted to 'abide in' God that they may not shrink in shame from the Christ at his appearing, and are reminded, 'If you know that he is righteous, you know that everyone who practises righteousness is born of him' (2.29). Indeed, we cannot stop at this point. For in the next chapter the τεκνία are exhorted, 'Let no one deceive you: he who does right is righteous, as he is righteous', and instruction is given to them as to how the children of God may be distinguished from the children of the devil (3.7–18). The following chapter describes the manifestation of the spirit of Antichrist in the world and contains the observation, 'τεκνία, you are of God and have overcome them (!); for he who is in you is greater than he who is in the world' (4.4). But it is surely plain already in 2.1 ('τεκνία, I am writing this to you so that you may not sin') and confirmed by the concluding saying of the Letter ('τεκνία, keep yourselves from idols', 5.21) that τεκνία is simply a favourite term of the writer for 'the children of God', i.e. for Christians generally. I know no modern New Testament scholar who disputes this, and I am frankly perplexed as to how exegesis of the kind we have considered finds its way in a twentieth-century theological report; I hope I may be forgiven for suggesting that the treatment of these New Testament sayings concerning 'children' provides an acute example of the manner in which some of our greatest theologians falter and lose their sure footing when they try to discover infant baptism in the Bible.

In fairness it must be admitted that what has been cited so far is overshadowed by the larger theological issues with which the reports deal. We find in them a particularly fine insistence on the priority of God in redemption, an emphasis which, it is urged, is clearly represented in baptism. The application of this emphasis, however, is apt at times to become tendentious. For example, baptism is described as 'a sacrament of the

---

[1] p. 19. It is, of course, a reflection of Stauffer's idea of the *oikos*-formula.

Incarnation and the new creation in Christ', i.e. of our incorporation in Christ and entry into the new creation. That is undoubtedly of utmost importance and has been insufficiently recognized; but the writers conclude from this, 'In baptism all men are alike, because their one qualification for baptism is their membership in this sinful humanity which Christ has redeemed.'[1] As a general statement that is unexceptionable, but if it is intended to imply that no condition or limiting circumstance is to be observed in the administration of baptism, what possible objection can be raised to the use of a hose in mass baptisms? In fact there is no Church which administers baptism without limiting conditions, not even the Church of Scotland, and the Apostles did not behave otherwise.

The doctrine of baptism in relation to the covenant is similarly presented. In the giving of the covenant the emphasis is naturally on the divine side: 'In the new covenant, in all our preaching and baptizing, it is Christ who has already fulfilled the covenant in Himself, and completed the work of our deliverance, who begins our faith and brings it to completion,'[2] an admirable statement. It is then urged, 'Our salvation ultimately depends upon something other than our faithfulness within the covenant relationship: that would be a salvation by works, and who then would be saved? . . . The ground of baptism is therefore not our faith, but the faithfulness of Christ.'[3] Who, indeed, would wish to maintain otherwise? All this, however, provides a suitable context for the assertion, 'The New Testament appears to take it for granted that infants are to be initiated into the new covenant as they were into the old.'[4] The declaration of Acts 2.39, 'The promise is to you and to your children' is cited in proof of this: 'Here we have an unequivocal insistence that children come within the Covenant and that the promise of the Spirit in baptism is for them too.'[5] The saying about the holy children in I Cor. 7.14 also finds its pertinence in this connection: 'Either "holy" refers to baptized children who are given the Holy Spirit . . . or it refers to children of the baptized, because they already participate in their parent's (or parents') baptismal incorporation into the Holy People'; but since the New Testament does not know two classes of Christians, the baptized and the born Christians, 'we are forced to conclude that if "holy" does not refer to baptized children, the fact that they are "holy", that they are already within the Holy People, the New Israel, demands their baptism.'[6]

I am sure that not a few theologians who sympathize with much of this

---

[1] *The Biblical Doctrine of Baptism*, Edinburgh, 1958, pp. 42 f.
[2] *Op. cit.*, p. 58.   [3] *Ibid.*   [4] p. 45.
[5] *1955 Report*, p. 21.   [6] p. 27.

thinking will yet find difficulty in representing it as the *biblical* doctrine of baptism, to cite the title of the popularized report. The term 'biblical' is ambiguous, for while it commonly denotes the actual thought of the writers of the Bible, it can be used for thinking that is congruous with the Bible, but the two cannot be equated. The doctrine of the ministry in the New Testament is varied and comparatively undeveloped, though on the way to fuller explication, but we are all aware of the difficulty of determining what is and what is not 'congruous with the Bible' in the varied traditions of ministry in the Churches. Similarly, while there may be sound warrant for applying the covenant idea to baptism, to claim that its exposition by the Scottish divines represents what the Apostles and Evangelists were trying to say is another matter. One has but to read Paul's most extensive exposition of the significance of the 'covenant' in Gal. 3 to appreciate the difficulty. The Apostle teaches that the covenant with Abraham remained in force during the era of Law, but none could receive the inheritance under it; in Christ however, it has been actualized. To the question *how* men may enter the covenant and become its heirs, a clear answer is given: *in baptism by faith*. 'It is men of faith who are the sons of Abraham . . . that in Christ Jesus the blessing of Abraham might come upon the Gentiles, that we might receive the promise of the Spirit through faith. . . . The scripture consigned all things to sin, that what was promised to faith in Jesus Christ might be given to those who believe. . . . Before faith came we were confined under the law, kept under restraint until faith should be revealed; so that the law was our custodian until Christ came, that we might be justified by faith. . . . For in Christ Jesus you are all sons of God through faith, for as many of you as were baptized to Christ did put on Christ' (vv. 7.14, 22 ff., 26 f.). The traditional idea of the covenant operating on a kind of hereditary basis is excluded by these statements. If Paul had shared the so-called covenant theology as expounded by the Scottish divines he could never have written this chapter of Galatians.

At this juncture we can go no further. Most of the issues touched on in this review will be discussed in detail in the main body of the book. It must be recognized, however, that the present work is not really concerned with the theology of infant baptism, still less is it written as a plea to jettison infant baptism. It sets into focus a single issue: *Is infant baptism found and expounded in the New Testament?* The theologians of the Church of England give a negative answer, the Church of Scotland theologians still answer in the affirmative; and both Churches practise infant baptism! Is then the question a purely academic one? By no means. If the baptism of the New Testament Church was that of responsible persons, the question arises whether the New Testament baptismal theology can be applied to infants and if so to what extent and under what conditions. W. F. Flemington, a Methodist, affirmed; 'It cannot be too strongly emphasized that many of the difficulties about the doctrine of baptism arise because statements of St Paul and others in the New Testament about *adult* baptism as they knew it in the first century AD are applied, without modification, to *infant* baptism as most Christian communions know it today.'[1] This issue has been curiously ignored by most Continental writers on baptism, whereas it has considerably occupied the Anglican theologians. It appears to demand more realistic thinking on the part of the theologians of the great Churches than has yet been accorded it. To this and like questions the present volume serves as a prolegomenon; their discussion must be pursued elsewhere.

Spurgeon's College   G. R. BEASLEY-MURRAY
London

[1] *The New Testament Doctrine of Baptism*, London, 1948, p. 82.

I

Changes

IT IS perhaps not unimportant that at the commencement of our investigations we should briefly pass in review what the last generation thought about the practice of infant baptism in the age of the New Testament and in the early period of the Church. Only then can we fully appreciate the change of opinion which our time has witnessed. As late as 1924 Adolf Harnack summarized his own view and that of many others as though he were stating a forgone conclusion: 'The practice of infant baptism begins after this period (the end of the second century). At least, we cannot certainly verify it earlier.'[1] In a footnote he complements this statement by a negation: 'To me it seems certain that the saying is applicable to this matter: "*ab initio sic non erat*".'[2] Now Harnack was an adherent of the 'liberal theology'; could that theology by chance have been responsible for such a judgment? Scarcely, for if we interrogate one who was certainly proof against such temptations, namely Paul Feine, and ask about his view, we find him explaining it even more emphatically as self-evident: 'The practice of infant baptism is not demonstrable in the Apostolic and post-Apostolic age. It is true that we hear frequently of the baptism of whole households, e.g. Acts 16.15, 32 f., 18.8, I Cor. 1.16. But the last passage taken in conjunction with I Cor. 7.14 does not tell in favour of the view that infant baptism was usual at that time. For in that case Paul could not have written: ἐπεὶ ἄρα τὰ τέκνα ὑμῶν ἀκάθαρτά ἐστιν.'[3]

These citations suffice to illustrate the view of a former generation. Let us go a step farther, to the time immediately prior to the present discussion. In 1931 Ethelbert Stauffer wrote the article on 'Baptism in Primitive Christianity' for the second edition of the encyclopaedia, *Religion in Geschichte und Gegenwart*. Here Stauffer, who today passionately defends the existence

---

[1] *Die Mission und Ausbreitung des Christentums in den ersten drei Jahrhunderten*⁴, 1924, I, p. 399; cf. ET, *The Expansion of Christianity . . .*², 1908, I, pp. 388 f.

[2] *Ibid.*, n. 2 (ET, p. 389 n. 1).

[3] *Realencyklopaedie für protestantische Theologie und Kirche*, 3rd ed., Vol. 19, 1907, p. 403.

of infant baptism in New Testament times,[1] affirmed: 'The baptism of infants is nowhere [in the New Testament] mentioned.'[2] 'Manifestly he [Paul] does not yet know of infant baptism; at all events his statement in I Cor. 7.14 as to the sanctification of children through their parents speaks against it.'[3] According to Paul baptism in the Gentile churches is 'constantly thought of as for adults. While the presuppositions and motives of infant baptism are comprehensible enough, and its beginnings gradually became perceptible, as yet no notice is taken of it (apart from Tertullian, *De bapt.* 18). Baptism is intended to be an end and a new beginning.'[4] Stauffer goes so far as to cast doubt on the practice of baptizing adults in the time of Jesus. He writes: 'From the moment that the Baptist disappears we hear not a word in any Gospel of any kind of baptism. Even in the mission charge, which is detailed on many matters, Jesus says nothing about baptism. Apparently Jesus does not continue the baptism of John, nor does he set another kind of baptism in its place.'[5] 'Christian baptism seems to have begun abruptly after the events of Easter.'[6]

Shortly after this the development began, the last stage of which may be seen in the work of Joachim Jeremias, *Infant Baptism in the first Four Centuries*, published in German in 1958 and in English in 1960. The English edition naturally represents a translation of the German, but it differs from it through a series of omissions and additions. A brief resumé of the conclusions to which these two editions have led must now be given, in the connection and order that Jeremias has chosen to follow. The English edition will be treated as basic, since it is the later one. Only where the two editions differ will the German edition also be cited. A summary report of this kind is necessary, first to make clear the nature of the changes that have taken place in the last forty years, which virtually amount to a reversal of the conclusions of the previous generation, and also because it will not be possible to adhere throughout our investigation to the order of thought adopted by Jeremias. On methodological grounds the investigation must be pursued in a different manner from that of Jeremias. His arguments and interpretations, of course, must be fully reviewed. It is but fair to let Jeremias speak for himself before entering on a discussion with him, and it may help the reader of this book to have a connected outline of Jeremias' interpretation at the very beginning.

'The early history of infant baptism is much more clearly defined today than in any previous age'; so Jeremias characterizes the situation today.[7]

---

[1] We shall later consider his position, since Jeremias appeals to Stauffer; cf. pp. 92 ff.
[2] *RGG*², Vol. V, Col. 1006.   [3] Cols. 1007 f.   [4] Col. 1009.
[5] Col. 1004.   [6] Col. 1005.   [7] Preface, p. 9.

He makes a point of departure in the distinction between 'the baptism of
children joining the Church'[1] and 'the baptism of children born to Christian parents'.[2] This distinction is encountered time and again. It is far
more than a terminological refinement, it denotes rather a pivotal point in
the argument of Jeremias: 'If we do not carefully distinguish these two
questions we shall make it impossible for ourselves to get a clear historical
view of the earliest times.'[3] Accordingly he begins with a consideration of
'missionary baptism'[4] in New Testament times. In keeping with the
mission situation of this age, all the utterances of the New Testament relate to this missionary baptism. In the view of Jeremias this explains why
'in the New Testament statements about baptism, the conversion of adults
and their baptism stands right in the middle of the picture,'[5] and why there
is nowhere any explicit mention of a baptism of children. Nevertheless (he
urges) it may be certainly inferred from the statements of the New Testament that children who were members of families going over to Christianity (irrespective of whether they came from heathenism or from Judaism)
were baptized together with their parents. The New Testament speaks in
various places of the conversion and baptism of whole 'houses'. Admittedly
the baptism of children, or of very little children, is not mentioned in these
passages; but since the technical term οἶκος can also be reproduced as
ὅλος ὁ οἶκος, πᾶς ὁ οἶκος, οἱ αὐτοῦ ἅπαντες, additions of this order make
it 'quite clear' that 'no single member of the household was excluded from
baptism'.[6] In view of the social strata to which the oldest churches belonged, 'it is extremely unlikely that the households of Cornelius, of the
keeper of the prison in Philippi, of Lydia, of Crispus the leader of the
synagogue and of Stephanas ever included a considerable group of slaves,
to whom the words ὅλος, πᾶς, ἅπαντες could refer. Accordingly the natural
conclusion is that we should take these additional terms to refer to all the
children of the house.'[7] This conclusion is confirmed by Old Testament
terminology. E. Stauffer has investigated the Old Testament material—'a
task which, incredible to relate, no one had attempted before'—and come

---

[1] This the title of the first chapter, pp. 19–42.
[2] So runs the title of the second chapter, pp. 43–58, which is concerned with the New
Testament period; chapter three, pp. 59–86, continues the investigation into later times.
[3] p. 43. For further details on this see below, pp. 42 ff.
[4] Translator's note. *Übertrittstaufe*, a key term in this book, could well be rendered by
'conversion baptism', but this would be misleading since the latter is an excellent
equivalent of the βάπτισμα μετανοίας ('repentance baptism') of John, and there are at least
some who look for conversion among the 'people of God' even now! *Übertrittstaufe* is
viewed as applicable to converts from without; it denotes the baptism of those who in
this act 'step over' into the Church. I have followed David Cairns in rendering it
'missionary baptism'.
[5] p. 19.   [6] p. 20: on this see below, pp. 87 ff.   [7] *Ibid.*: on this see below, pp. 87 ff.

to the conclusion that 'from early times there was a constant biblical "*oikos*-formula" which "not only referred to the children in addition to the adults but had quite *special* references to the children, and not least to any *small children* who might be present".'[1] This 'New Testament *oikos*-formula' is very old. It occurs in Paul's writings as early as AD 54 and is found independently in Luke, hence it represents a 'pre-Pauline formula' and it 'comes from a time in which the majority of the members of the churches came from the synagogue and from the circle of the "God-fearers" loosely attached thereto'.[2] If this fact is grasped by us, we shall be compelled to agree with Stauffer's conclusion. Admittedly it is not stated that in every particular case where the baptism of an *oikos* is mentioned little children were present: 'but it does mean that Paul and Luke could under no circumstances have applied the *oikos*-formula, if they had wished to say that only adults had been baptized.'[3] It is also necessary to consider 'how great a part family solidarity played in the ancient world. . . . In particular in its relation to God the household was a unity.'[4] It is true that quite early there must have been mixed marriages, but when only one partner was converted it was the wife. 'When we consider family solidarity resting upon the authoritative influence of the head of the family it is scarcely conceivable that the baptism of a "household" did not include all its members.'[5] Since baptism was an eschatological sacrament, 'a division within the families joining the Church by reason of a difference of age is, in these circumstances, highly improbable.'[6] Jewish proselyte baptism, which according to *Test. Levi* 14.6 stretches back into pre-Christian times,[7] finally offers a 'multiplicity of contacts with primitive Christian baptism',[8] and they cannot be explained as 'accidental agreements'. In this matter 'the possibility of accidental analogies is wholly inconceivable; the only possible conclusion is that the rites are related as parent and child.'[9] Moreover, 'we must take into account the fact that especially in the East rites persist tenaciously even when their significance and interpretation alter. Accordingly when we seek clarification of the question whether the primitive Church baptized children as well as adults when they changed their religion, we shall have to give all the more weight to the corresponding procedure in relation to proselyte baptism.'[10] Here male infants were immediately circumcised on the entry of heathen families into Judaism, and girls were baptized. When boys were born after this conversion they were circumcised like Jewish boys on the eighth day, but if girls were born after the transference nothing was done to them,

---

[1] p. 20.   [2] p. 21.   [3] p. 22.   [4] *Ibid.*   [5] p. 23.   [6] *Ibid.*
[7] p. 26.   [8] p. 29: on this see below, pp. 83 f.   [9] p. 36.   [10] p. 37.

since they were reckoned as Jewish girls. It is to be presumed that 'in the question of infant baptism also the Christian baptismal ritual corresponded to that of proselyte baptism, i.e. that with the admission of Gentiles to Christianity children of every age, including infants, were baptized also.'[1] Since Paul in Col. 2.11 calls baptism 'Christian circumcision', this description 'makes it very probable that the procedure in baptism was the same, that is, that children of every age were baptized along with their parents when the latter were converted to the Christian faith'.[2] Individual testimonies, like Acts 2.38 f. and certain of the inscriptions, support this conclusion.[3]

According to Jeremias the position differed with the baptism of children born to Christian parents. Here 'we must reckon with the possibility that the practice was different in Jewish Christian circles from what it was in Gentile Christian circles, because here as there the practice was different with respect to circumcision.'[4] The Judaistic group of the primitive Church naturally had their own male children circumcised. 'Did they in addition have them baptized? Or were they content with circumcising them?'[5] Among the churches in the area of Paul's missionary activity circumcision was not practised. 'In the case of children of parents of Gentile birth we learn this from Gal. 5.2; in the case of children of parents of Jewish birth it is asserted in Acts 21.21. Was baptism, the "circumcision of Christ" (Col. 2.11), here a rite substituted for circumcision?'[6] So asks Jeremias. But whereas to this point his book in the English and German editions is almost identical, the two editions go apart from now on to the end of the chapter.[7] The same building materials are used but they are differently arranged and they form different constructions. It will be advisable to give an account of both series of arguments alongside and after each other.

In the German edition of 1958 Jeremias adduces as testimonies for the earliest period I Cor. 7.14c[8] and Acts 21.21.[9] The 'change of practice' is set forth by a series of *argumenta e silentio*, by allusions to Origen, the D-text of Acts 2.39 and Tertullian, as also with the aid of the Zosimos and Alkinoos inscriptions from the third century. The *pericope* Mark 10.13-16, which is expounded in a separate section,[10] affords 'an indirect allusion to a

---

[1] p. 39. [2] pp. 39 f.
[3] These are discussed below in detail, pp. 75 ff., and therefore are merely mentioned here. [4] p. 43.
[5] *Ibid*. And, we might add this question here, what did they do with the girls, to whom nothing was done in Judaism?
[6] pp. 43 f. [7] In the English edition, pp. 44-58; in the German, pp. 57-68.
[8] pp. 51-56 of the German edition. [9] pp. 56 f., German ed.
[10] pp. 57-61, German ed.

C

terminus ante quem when the Church in the middle fifties of the first century ceased the practice that had hitherto existed of withholding baptism from Christian children.'[1] Jeremias affirmed as a result of his argument at that time: 'Thus the apostolic Church between AD 60 and 70 took the step of baptizing not only children of converts, whom she had baptized from the beginning, but also the children who were born in the Church—and indeed as infants!'[2] For in his judgment both the Pauline churches and the earliest church in Jerusalem originally did not baptize the children of Christian families. In Corinth not only the children of mixed marriages but the children of all Christian marriages were not baptized, because they were born 'in holiness'. Undoubtedly, adds Jeremias, the inference from I Cor. 7.14c, 'Paul appears . . . to know nothing of the baptism of Christian born to Christian parents,'[3] can only be drawn 'with real reserve'.[4] 'Nevertheless,' he continues, 'it is confirmed from quite another side.'[5] For I Cor. 7.14 makes use of late Jewish ritual terminology. In later Judaism children who were born after the conversion of the mother to Judaism did not undergo the baptism of cleansing because they were born 'in holiness'. Hence, according to the view of Jeremias at that time, 'Both the context and the linguistic usage' lead to the conclusion that 'in AD 54 in Corinth, children born to Christian parents were not baptized'.[6]

In the English edition of 1960 Jeremias expounds I Cor. 7.14 in almost the same manner: 'We conclude that the holiness of the children rests not on baptism, but on their descent from a Christian father or a Christian mother.'[7] He emphasizes this statement by adding, 'This is today generally recognized.'[8] In a fresh paragraph he affirms the difficulty of believing that there existed in Corinth a special doctrine about the holiness of children of mixed marriages. Paul's argument is explicable only from the assumption 'that not only the children of a mixed marriage but all the children in the fellowship were counted holy, because they came of Christian parents'.[9] The statements about the parallelism between I Cor. 7.14 and late Jewish ritual terminology are repeated. But then Jeremias continues, 'One would be tempted at first to draw the following conclusion: "If in later Judaism children born 'in holiness' were not baptized, then we must assume that the Christian Church also forebore to baptize the children of Christian parents. In this case children born before their parents joined the Church would have been baptized, but not those born 'in holiness'. "'[10] So he had argued as recently as the German edition. Now

---

[1] pp. 61–68, German ed. [2] p. 61, German ed. [3] p. 54, German ed.
[4] *Ibid.*   [5] *Ibid.*   [6] p. 56, German ed. [7] p. 54.
[8] p. 45 n. 1.   [9] p. 45.   [10] p. 47.

however he has 'begun to doubt the validity of this reasoning'.[1] For it overlooks 'the important fact' that all boys were circumcised on the eighth day, irrespective as to whether they were born 'in holiness' or not. 'Since, as Col. 2.11 f.[2] tells us, in the Christian Church baptism was the rite which replaced circumcision, we must conclude that the fact that the children mentioned in I Cor. 7.14c were "holy" from their birth does not preclude the possibility that they were baptized.'[3] Even in the case of an unbelieving partner in a mixed marriage baptism after conversion was a necessity.[4] Jeremias accordingly renounces any desire to draw conclusions about the baptism of children in the Pauline churches. 'We must be content with the conclusion that I Cor. 7.14c bears no reference to baptism. There is every probability that the statement, "For your children are holy," no more excluded the baptism of children on the eighth day, in place of circumcision, than the saying, "Your unbelieving husband is holy," excluded the later baptism of the husband. But here we cannot get beyond conjecture.'[5]

Acts 21.21 in both editions is interpreted in the same manner; it is affirmed that the primitive Church in Jerusalem about AD 55 circumcised the male children born in its midst. In both editions Jeremias raises the question whether these boys also received baptism; the Donatist Cresconius c. AD 400 reported that the dual observance was maintained by the so-called Symmachians, and the Coptic and the Abyssinian Churches to this day continue both customs. Jeremias in the German edition of 1958 gives as his answer to the question: 'We do not know. Nevertheless in the light of the evidence adduced on pp. 54–56 [concerning I Cor. 7.14c and the Corinthians withholding baptism from children] we must presume it to be improbable that the highly legalistic Jewish Christians of Jerusalem made their children born "in holiness" to undergo baptism as well as circumcision; with due reserve we must conclude that in Jerusalem about AD 55 children born of Christians were not baptized. The fact that we were able to establish that in the year earlier a like withholding from baptism took place in Corinth supports this conclusion and justifies the generalization that about the middle of the first century AD children born of Christian parents, both in Jewish Christian and heathen Christian areas, in all probability were not baptized. As children of believing parents they were born "in holiness" and therefore occupied a place in the sphere of salvation and the realm of Christ's grace.'[6] In the English edition of 1961 Jeremias leaves the question unanswered and continues: 'At the same time, we

[1] *Ibid.*
[2] On this see further, p. 84.
[3] p. 47.
[4] pp. 47 f.
[5] p. 48.
[6] p. 57, German ed.

learn from Acts 21.21 that in Pauline territory parents of Jewish (and all the more of heathen) descent did not have their male children circumcised on the eighth day after birth. Since Paul designates baptism as the ritual which replaces circumcision (Col. 2.11), it is very probable that these children were baptized.'[1]

This conclusion, he believes, is supported by Mark 10.13–16. In 1958 the passage was adduced as proof for the practice of infant baptism; in the later edition it strengthens the chain of proof of this much more closely knit chapter, which cites I Cor. 7.14c and Acts 21.21 (in the manner just described) as giving 'grounds for judging how the earliest age dealt with children born to Christian parents'.[2] The treatment of the Marcan *pericope* in the 1961 edition essentially corresponds to that of 1958, so that it is needless to recount it here in detail; a full statement is given on pp. 95 ff. in the discussion of Jeremias' interpretation of the narrative and its parallels. Likewise the two inscriptions that Jeremias brings forward in the section entitled 'Special Evidence' do not require discussion at this point, since that will be given when the other inscriptions are considered.[3] At this juncture we are only concerned with the general grounds with which Jeremias supports his new thesis, that the Church from the beginning applied infant baptism to children born in Christian families.[4] The necessity for such support is illustrated by the admission that Jeremias is compelled to make, despite all the arguments that have gone before: 'For the first century we have no special evidence for the baptism of Christian children.'[5]

Five arguments are brought forward by Jeremias to assist his case: 1. 'We hear in the history of the early Church nothing about two kinds of Christians, baptized and unbaptized; had baptism been withheld from children born to Christian parents, then there would very soon have grown up a mixed crowd of baptized and unbaptized Christians living alongside of each other.'[6] 2. Nowhere in the literature of the ancient Church do we find any discussion on the question whether children of Christian parents ought to be baptized; rather it appears, in the light of all we know, that the custom of later times goes back without any break to that of the earlier. 'Had the custom of baptizing them not been introduced until the second century, it would have been quite inconceivable that the introduction of so startling a novelty would have left no trace in the sources, which begin to be more abundant at this time.'[7] 3. The custom of baptizing children must

---

[1] p. 48. [2] p. 44. [3] See below, pp. 75 ff.
[4] They occur in the same wording in the German edition, although in another context.
[5] p. 55. [6] p. 57. [7] p. 57.

have begun early. 'Had the practice not been introduced until a time when the baptismal ritual had reached a rather fuller state of development, the Church would surely not have been content simply to apply the ritual of adult baptism to children.'[1] 4. Infant baptism nowhere appears as the special doctrine of a Church group or sect. 'What we have before us is rather one of the few Church usages in relation to which the great Church everywhere was completely unanimous. Even Tertullian shares this unanimity; however lively, at least on occasion, may have been his plea for the postponement of the baptism of children of pagans joining the Church, he took the baptism of Christian children for granted.'[2] 5. East and West are one in believing that infant baptism goes back to the time of the Apostles, hence this tradition ought not to be lightly set aside. For the Gospel of John could scarcely have formulated in so unqualified a manner the proposition that only those begotten by water and the spirit can enter the kingdom of God (John 3.5), if in its time baptism had been withheld from children of Christian parents.'[3]

The remaining investigations of the book are given over to considering 'the development up to the end of the third century'.[4] Jeremias begins with the East, 'for which the evidence is more scanty',[5] wanders through its provinces and at length reaches the West, 'which provides more material'.[6] Asia Minor offers us in the statements of Polycarp, Polycrates, the Letter of Pliny and the Acts of the Martyrs indirect evidence as to the length of time during which certain individuals were members of the Church,[7] and so, in Jeremias' view, of their baptism at a very early age. With the aid of the oldest of them Jeremias is able to reach back 'to apostolic times, probably to the years when the Gospels of Matthew and Luke were written'.[8] For Egypt Jeremias pays only passing attention to Clement of Alexandria,[9] but he accords a more detailed treatment to Origen, whose testimony is 'of the greatest importance'.[10] His contributions 'were written between 233 and 251, but they take us back to a considerably earlier period'.[11] For if Origen speaks of infant baptism as 'a tradition handed down from the Apostles', he could hardly have done so 'had he not known that at least his father and probably also his grandfather had been baptized as παιδία. This means that the tradition of his family carries us back from the date of his own baptism at least to the date of his father's— i.e. to the middle of the second century, and probably even to the baptism of his grandfather in the first half of that century.'[12] Indeed, Jeremias

[1] *Ibid.* [2] *Ibid.* [3] p. 58.
[4] The title of the third chapter, pp. 59–86. [5] p. 58. [6] *Ibid.*
[7] For further details, see below, pp. 70 ff. [8] p. 59. [9] On this see below, pp. 59 f.
[10] On this see below, pp. 47 ff. [11] p. 66. [12] *Ibid.*

advances a stage further: 'He could not have talked in so unqualified a manner of infant baptism as 'the custom of the Church' (*ecclesiae observantia*) if in his journeys he had come on deviations in practice within the sphere of the Great Church. Thus his witness holds good for practically the whole eastern Church of his time.'[1] An illustration of the practice of infant baptism in Egypt in that period is provided by the clay coffin of a mummified Egyptian child, coming from the period *c.* AD 200 and now in the British Museum. On the coffin the dead child is portrayed as holding a lotus flower in the left hand, and in the right a cross affixed to a chain which is twice wound round the body. 'It is certain that we have here an example of Egyptian syncretism of the third century AD'[2] (the dead wears the beard of Osiris, etc.). Moreover, since 'heathen mummies in many cases hold the symbol of life in their right hands', one could possibly speak here of a 'Christianized *ankh*-sign'.[3] The estimates of the age of the mummy varied among the Egyptologists between eighteen months and ten years. But since Jeremias saw in the Egyptian Museum in Cairo a mummy of 80 centimetres long, which he would estimate from the portrait on it at four years of age, and the mummy in the British Museum is 74 centimetres long, he considers it to be somewhat younger. The cross which was 'placed in the right hand in the hour of death,[4] shows that she was a Christian child. And so in view of the evidence of Origen as to the practice of infant baptism in the Egyptian Church of that time, we must assume that the little girl was baptized.'[5]

Certain statements of Origen afford Jeremias evidence of the practice of infant baptism in Palestine and West Syria, and a passage from the Pseudo-Clementines adds further proof for West Syria (the work belongs to the fourth century but the original writing is to be dated AD 220–230). Nevertheless 'the first direct evidence for the practice of infant baptism in Syria is given by Asterius the Sophist (died after 341) and the *Apostolic Constitutions* (370–380).'[6] As to East Syria, it is certain that infant baptism had not long been known in the area: 'There is no trace of evidence that

---

[1] p. 70.   [2] p. 67.   [3] p. 67.
[4] ?? This seems to me to be read into the facts, just as many questions remain open in connection with this clay coffin, interesting though it be (it will not be later discussed). Even if the estimate of the age of the child by Jeremias as 'somewhat younger' than four years be correct, and his interpretation of the characteristics of the dead be admitted, no contribution to our theme is thereby gained. We do not know when this child was baptized, assuming that it was baptized. If it took place, as in numerous similar cases (cf. the Christian inscriptions, pp. 75 ff.) as an emergency baptism shortly before death, we then have a proof of a situation which is to be met elsewhere. If we were to grant the entire hypothesis of Jeremias as proven, and indeed go beyond the actual assertions of Jeremias and assume that the dead child had been baptized as an infant, we have but an illustration of the practice of infant baptism at the beginning of the third century or end of the second century, which is already attested by Tertullian.   [5] p. 78.   [6] p. 69.

here infant baptism was practised in the first centuries.'[1] Marcionite and other influences[2] played a role in this quarter.

In the West Jeremias finds in the *Apology of Aristides* 15.11 a passage which, 'rightly understood',[3] provides an 'indirect proof' for the use of infant baptism at the beginning of the second century.[4] For Italy and Gaul a piece of evidence from Justin[5] and the correction of Acts 2.39 in Codex Bezae[6] afford Jeremias indirect allusions to infant baptism, but Irenaeus[7] expressly attests infant baptism as an 'unquestioned practice of the Church'.[8] Still more important, however, is the testimony of the *Church Order* of Hippolytus, which possesses 'the same outstanding significance for the West'[9] as that of Origen for the East. As to the original Greek form of this work many questions remain open; only a few fragments of it are extant, and we have to reconstruct it from traditions handed down in other languages, which understandably raises many difficult problems. Nevertheless Jeremias accepts it not only as evidence for the time of its origin ('about 215')[10] but also for earlier generations: 'It would be a mistake if we were to reckon the work merely as evidence for the beginning of the third century. For Hippolytus, who probably incorporated the *Church Order* into his book Περὶ χαρισμάτων ἀποστολικὴ παράδοσις as its second part, had no intention of introducing new rules for Church action, but as the title of his work indicates, of setting down the older ("apostolic") tradition. And this is true also of infant baptism.'[11] For Jeremias' interpretation of the *Church Order* of Hippolytus the assumption that we here deal with the entry of converts into the Christian Church[12] is of importance (though he does not discuss it). After a detailed consideration of burial inscriptions relating to Christian children[13] ('noting in passing that there are no Christian epitaphs earlier than AD 200'),[14] Jeremias turns to Africa, i.e. especially Tertullian and Cyprian. The picture which Jeremias draws of Tertullian's teaching on infant baptism is contradictory, although we cannot discuss the grounds for this statement at this juncture.[15] In his writing *De paenitentia* Tertullian, according to Jeremias, opposes 'the tendency to postpone joining the Church, because of the belief that in view of the forgiveness to be expected in baptism one could continue in sin until baptism without worrying'.[16] In his work composed about the same time, *De baptismo*, it is 'all the more astonishing' that Tertullian 'advocated . . . postponement of baptism in special cases'. Jeremias

---

[1] *Ibid.* [2] On this cf. below, p. 101. [3] p. 71.
[4] For further details on this see below, pp. 57 f. [5] See further, pp. 73 f.
[6] See further, pp. 85 f. [7] See further, pp. 58 f.
[8] p. 73: the phrase is cited from Windisch. [9] p. 73. [10] p. 74. [11] *Ibid.* [12] p. 75.
[13] On this see further, pp. 75 ff. [14] p. 75. [15] On this see further, pp. 61 ff. [16] p. 81.

explains: 'In order to understand this passage we must take into account that the tract *De baptismo*, like so many other tracts of Tertullian, was written to meet a special occasion. It seems to have had its origin in addresses to Carthaginian catechumens and neophytes. This means, however, that in the whole tract Tertullian has primarily the baptism of converts in view.'[1] Tertullian's doubts about the baptism of children 'refer accordingly to the children of pagans joining the Church'.[2] His interpretation of Tertullian's tract *De anima* leads Jeremias to affirm, 'The reservations expressed in *De baptismo* 18 were not extended by Tertullian to cover the baptism of the children of Christian parents; perhaps he had gone so far as to drop them altogether.'[3] Cyprian[4] on the other hand presents no problems. Among his letters is mentioned a synodal decision from the time shortly after AD 250; from it we learn that in the judgment of the bishops baptism should be administered to a newborn child within three days at the most after birth, and even a postponement to the eighth day is to be rejected. From another passage we further gather that at that time little children received communion, 'which of course presupposes that they were baptized'.[5] The discussion of two inscriptions from North Africa[6] forms the conclusion of this section, which Jeremias summarizes by declaring, 'The inscriptions, which begin in the West about 200, confirm in detail the picture supplied by the literary sources.'[7]

'In the fourth century there occurred a great crisis in the matter of infant baptism.'[8] To this theme the closing chapter of the volume is devoted. Not only did Constantine the Great postpone baptism to his death-bed,[9] but children born to Christian parents were also, in part at least, not baptized till later years. Among such are to be numbered some prominent Christians, or members of prominent Christian families, e.g. Basil the Great, Ambrose, Chrysostom, Jerome, Rufinus, Paulinus of Nola, etc. 'These later very famous theologians, born between 329 and 354, were thus one and all brought up as Christians but not at first baptized.'[10] Jeremias indicates his view in the summary statement: 'Of great importance, not only for dating the crisis of infant baptism, but also for the history of baptism in general, is the fact that the earliest case known to us

---

[1] p. 82. For Jeremias it is an embarrassing fact that *De paenitentia* was written for the same circles of addressees and therefore similarly speaks of 'missionary baptism'; his interests are above all directed to prove that Tertullian either had no objection at all against the baptism of infants born in Christian families or he speedily dispelled his hesitations about it.   [2] p. 83.   [3] p. 85.   [4] See further on this, p. 46.
[5] p. 85.   [6] See further on this, p. 75.   [7] p. 85.   [8] p. 87.
[9] According to the categories of Jeremias this also is a 'missionary baptism', i.e. a continuation—if an extreme one—of the attitude which he finds in Tertullian's *De paenitentia*.   [10] p. 89.

in which Christian parents postponed the baptism of their children, is in the year 329–330 (Gregory of Nazianzus).'[1] On inscriptions from the fourth century the title 'neophyte' is found with respect to some who were baptized immediately before death. Jeremias adduces nine dated inscriptions belonging to the period 348–402; the age of the children ranges between eight months and nine years (six of the nine children are between five and nine years old). 'In so far as they are children of Christian parents, they are instances of a delay in baptism,'[2] he explains (naturally on the basis of his presuppositions). 'A more eloquent testimony than that of the direct evidence to the gravity and depth of the crisis is borne by the singular behaviour of the theologians,' he declares. 'They are silent. Not that they opposed the practice of infant baptism—of that we have not the slightest evidence. But no one has a clear policy in face of the crisis. In the critical decades after 330 Asterius the Sophist is the only theologian who attests, enjoins and argues for the baptism of the infant children of Christian parents. It is characteristic that so late as 370 Basil the Great and soon afterwards his younger brother, Gregory of Nyssa, while criticizing sharply people who go on postponing baptism, both have adults in mind and do not say a word about infant baptism, although it is reported of Basil that he was ready to baptize children *in extremis*.'[3] Jeremias asks whether the attitude of Basil was by chance determined by the fact that he himself had received baptism as an adult.[4] In face of the circumstances that 'for the first two-thirds of this century (as also for the second half of the third century) there is an almost complete lack of patristic evidence for infant baptism,'[5] he emphasizes (rightly) that one should not proceed to the conclusion that infant baptism was not practised at all in that time. He brings forward evidence to the contrary, which leads him to affirm, 'At the same time and in the same country for which we have reliable evidence for the postponement of baptism . . . we find the baptism of newborn infants as the normal practice.'[6] On this no further comment is needed. After the controversies of Augustine with the Pelagians, any objection to the rightness of infant baptism is impossible. By that time it has manifestly won a decisive victory.

[1] p. 89. [2] p. 90. [3] p. 91.
[4] The same is true of Gregory Nazianzus, who in the year 381 exhorts parents to have their children baptized (*Oratio* 40), although (as the son of a bishop!) he himself was baptized when about thirty years of age. [5] p. 91. [6] p. 93.

2

The First clear Testimonies for the Practice of Infant Baptism in the Third Century

THE LAST sentence of the previous chapter does not come from Jeremias —he would have formulated it differently—but it does indicate in which direction his thoughts go. This resumé of his position, which I have strenuously sought to present objectively, will already have made the attentive reader aware that various elements in the apparently unbroken chain of proof do not agree. Not infrequently hypotheses are employed which are first recognized as such, but in the course of the treatise they unnoticeably develop into established facts by which other hypotheses are supported, and these too suffer the same fate. Unproven presuppositions are utilized and are taken as self-evident, although they are nothing of the sort. In many cases this may be due to the fact that Jeremias starts with the New Testament and then pushes on into later centuries, which are nevertheless determined by quite different presuppositions.

Let us take as an example the assumption of crucial importance to Jeremias, that a distinction is to be drawn between 'missionary baptism' and the baptism of a child born of Christian parents. This idea of a 'missionary baptism' i.e. of someone coming into Christianity from heathendom or from Judaism, is drawn from the narratives of the New Testament. Here apparently we are confronted with the sudden conversion of a man moved by the mission preaching, who decisively turns from the old way of life and turns to the new and confirms the change through baptism. Now even for New Testament times considerable doubt is aroused as to whether baptism regularly followed 'conversion' at once. At least a rudimentary baptismal instruction may well have been a condition for baptism (cf. e.g. Acts 16.32, where even under the presupposition of the turbulent events of the night in the prison of Philippi the instruction of the prison warder is firmly adhered to). The more time passed, the more will the distance between adherence to the Christian Church and full reception into it through baptism have increased. Our oldest text outside the New Testament, so far as our theme is concerned, the *Didache*, says nothing of the way and the manner in which baptismal instruction was given and how long it lasted—chapters 1–6 give us simply the scheme or summary of what was taught in a text recited immediately prior to baptism. When we consider chapter 12, however, with its instructions for the reception of travelling guests from other Christian communities, it becomes plain that the churches at the turn of the first century AD were decidedly circumspect towards those who were without. In *Didache* 12 it states that every Christian should be welcomed if he requests the hospitality of his Christian brethren, but he should be tested as to the genuineness of his Christian standing. He should be treated as a guest at the most for two or three days; if he desires to remain longer he ought to provide for himself by work, and so on. Similar critical caution prevails with regard to visiting church officers from elsewhere and itinerant teachers and prophets (chapters 11 and 13); it is hardly imaginable therefore that new converts were immediately received as full members of the Church through baptism without first making them go through a period of probation.

In the moment that it does happen, however, 'missionary baptism' changes its character. It is no longer something 'from without'; it signifies the recognition of one who already belongs to the wider circle of the Church, who not only assents to the rightness of the teaching and the ethical prescriptions of Christianity but has already demonstrated this affirmation. In Justin (*Apol.* I.61) this situation is confirmed by an explicit statement: a time of probation precedes baptism; baptism is the seal upon instruction already given and vows already taken to live for the faith already recognized as true. The declaration of Justin reflects the usage about 150; nothing hinders us from assuming the like also for the preceding decades, indeed the tenor of the *Didache* compels us to it.[1] In the time that followed the same procedure holds good, as is evident from the increasing development of the institution of the catechumenate; the *Church Order* of Hippolytus (42.1 [xvii 1])[2] shortly after 200 lays down the normal length of this probationary period as three years. Here we learn with a wealth of detail something of the care exercised in the choice of

---

[1] The *Shepherd of Hermas* also speaks, in Visio III, 7.5, of a period prior to baptism of the proving and testing of a person seeking baptism.

[2] Cited according to the Coptic text and the numbering of the edition of W. Till and J. Leipoldt, *Der koptische Text der Kirchenordnung Hippolyts*, TU 58 (1954). [Translator's note: For the convenience of English readers the chapter and section of the reconstructed text of G. Dix, *ΑΠΟΣΤΟΛΙΚΗ ΠΑΡΑΔΟΣΙΣ, The Treatise on the Apostolic Tradition of St Hippolytus of Rome*, I (London, 1937), is added in square brackets.]

catechumens and how they virtually belonged to the Church, which had received them out of heathenism long before they became full Christians through submission to baptism. Prior to their admittance to the catechumenate a careful scrutiny of their former life takes place (40.2 [xvi 2]). Witnesses must give guarantee of the genuineness of their resolve and whether the applicants are 'in a condition to hear the Word' (40.3 [xvi 2]). Thus even before they become catechumens—in which condition they normally remain three years—they are acquainted with the basic elements of Christianity. The list of vocations and conditions which exclude the possibility of entering the catechumentate is long and particularly strict (40.4–41.17 [xvi 3–25]). During the catechumenate the catechumens attend the worship (43.1 [xviii 1]) and after the prayer they receive laying on of hands and are so dismissed (44.1 [xix 1]). The catechumens also participate in the communal meal, the bread of the oath is given to them (50.6 [xxvi 11]), or the bread of the oath and the cup (48.2 [xxvi 4]). They have to observe all the prescriptions of the Church Order exactly as the full Christians (62.23 [xxxvi 15]); hence in all respects they are full members of the Church, with the exception of participation in the eucharist and in the kiss of peace (43.2 [xviii 3]).

If that be so, then the so-called 'missionary baptism' is to a certain extent simply the door from the forecourt to the Most Holy Place; the newly baptized are already in the community of the Church, at least in the everyday life of the community, and are distinguished solely through exclusion from the eucharist. The Emperor Constantine was completely recognized as a Christian by the Church of his time, although he did not receive baptism and the Lord's Supper till his death-bed.[1] His son Constantius also received baptism only immediately before his death;[2] that did not hinder the catechumen from ruling the Church as the 'most Christian Emperor', nor the Church from acceding to his interventions in its innermost affairs and acclaiming his measures, as if this emperor had been a full Christian. Although Ambrose was a catechumen, he was elected by the Church of Milan as bishop, etc. If we now assume—for the moment only as a possibility—that children born of Christian marriages were not baptized immediately on birth but at a later point of time and after preliminary instruction, then the distinction between the children of those seeking baptism and the children of Christian parents is completely levelled out. The 'missionary baptism' postulated by Jeremias undoubtedly aids him to build up and extend his position—it permeates very con-

---

[1] Eusebius, *Vita Constantini*, IV, 61–64.
[2] Socrates, *HE*, II, 47.4; Philostorgius, *HE*, 6.5.

siderably his material in support of his argument.[1] Yet it seems to me that this distinction between 'missionary baptism' and the baptism of a child of Christian parents, although at first glance apparently illuminating, is a construction which does not come to terms with the actual situation of the churches of the second century, and in fact it is a distinction that never existed. But that will have to be established in the discussion of the sources. Moreover in the view of Jeremias the season when these 'missionary baptisms' took place is Easter. Yet the exclusive appointment of this season for 'missionary baptisms' is not mentioned in any source but is purely a postulate of Jeremias. It is quite certain that baptisms of children immediately before death took place without respect to the calendar, and Jeremias must, according to his theory, explain all such baptisms as 'missionary baptisms'. There is also no doubt that where infant baptism was introduced the Easter date was abandoned, not only in cases of clinical baptisms.[2] As for the Easter baptisms themselves, it is a point requiring to be proved that at those baptisms no children (of whatever age) of Christian parents were present.

One further observation before we consider the testimonies *seriatim*. It may appear to be merely a terminological matter, but in reality it signifies more. In the context of our theme we ought to cease speaking about the baptism of *children*.[3] Not only does the discussion become unclear when we do this, but the problem with which we are concerned is beclouded. Whoever discusses the baptism of children today actually means the baptism of *infants*, i.e. the baptism of newly-born children, either immediately

[1] Whereas Jeremias had originally accepted the view that in the time of Paul children born of Christian marriages were baptized neither in Gentile-Christian nor in Jewish-Christian churches, I Cor. 7.14c in his judgment is now excluded as evidence for the baptismal practice of the earliest generation. Similarly Acts 21.21 also now affords him no direct testimony for infant baptism in the primitive Jerusalem community; at best it can be evaluated for this purpose with the aid of Col. 2.11 (cf. p. 82). According to Jeremias the *Church Order* of Hippolytus speaks of 'missionary baptism'; so does Tertullian in *De baptismo*, and the majority of the inscriptions adduced by Jeremias; in that case what *direct* statements remain to him from the early times concerning the baptism in infancy of children born to Christian parents?

[2] Already in the *Church Order* of Hippolytus it is written (45.5 [xx 6]): 'When a woman is in the custom of women (= menstruation) she should be left and baptized on another day'. John Chrysostom (*Hom. in Acts* 1.7, 60.24) testifies for the fourth century that baptism was not bound to the Easter season, Maximum of Turin (= Augustine, *serm.* 210.2; MPL 38.1048) does the same for the fifth century, to mention but a few examples.

[3] Translator's note. The author is concerned with a difficulty of terminology common to many Continental ecclesiastical traditions but which has not affected the British. German speaking people generally do not speak of 'infant baptism' but of 'children's baptism', *Kindertaufe*, as the French use the ambiguous phrase 'le baptême des enfants' and the Scandinavians 'barndop'. Since an acceptable German expression for infant baptism exists, *Säuglingstaufe*, the author appeals that it should be used for the sake of clarity.

or a few weeks or months after birth, in contrast to a postponement of baptism, whether the delay be envisaged for but a few years till the attainment of some understanding, or for a longer time till the attainment of a 'full' understanding and the possibility of independent decision. When Jeremias discusses 'the baptism of children in the first four centuries', he naturally means the baptism of infants.[1] He is concerned to prove that this baptism of infants, even when they are the children of Christian parents, has continually been practised in the Church, and that exceptions to this rule are to be observed only in 'missionary baptisms'. An example from the sources will perhaps make plain the facts of the situation and the necessity for a more precise mode of expression. Gregory Nazianzus in his *Oratio* 40 of the year 381 counsels that children be baptized about the age of three years because then they are not only able to answer the baptismal questions themselves but also are in a position to understand the Christian faith, at least to some degree. Here we see an affirmation of the baptism of *children*, yet Gregory Nazianzus, by his mode of argument and the results to which it leads, must be ranged along with those who repudiate the present day practice of the Church, i.e. the baptism of infants immediately after birth. Only if we speak of the baptism of *infants* does the nature of the problem in the earliest days of the Church come clearly into focus, and only so can we gain an answer to the question we pose today. Jeremias logically reckons Gregory Nazianzus among those in whom 'a certain effect of the crisis of the fourth century is visible'.[2]

Indubitable testimonies for the practice of infant baptism in the Christian Church first begin in the third century; so we have laid down in the foreword and so we repeat in the title of this chapter. There are three witnesses or groups of witnesses with which we are concerned: the *Church Order* of Hippolytus, a synodal letter of Cyprian, and some utterances of Origen. The most unambiguous is the declaration of Cyprian and we therefore take it first. Shortly after AD 250, after consultation with the bishops of North Africa, he writes his *Epistle* 64 to Bishop Fidus in reply to a question which is no longer extant. The Carthaginian bishop expressly demands that the baptism of infants should take place on the second or third day after birth; the view of Fidus that they ought to wait until the eighth day, as with the parallel rite of circumsion,[3] is unanimously repudiated by all bishops. The argument adduced by Fidus, that children in the first days after their birth are too repulsive to give them the kiss of peace,[4] cannot bear examination, for to the pure all things are pure and no

---

[1] Cf. e.g., pp. 53 f., 74, etc.   [2] p. 96.
[3] *Ep.* 64.2 (CSEL 3.2, p. 718, ed. Hartel), Kraft no. 19a, p. 20.   [4] *Ep* 64.4, p. 719.

one should hinder the newly born from receiving grace. This is stated with such definiteness, we must conclude that infant baptism at this time in Africa was not only a Church rule but a Church requirement. It includes also the baptism of children of Christian parents and so in every respect is a completely valid testimony.

The case is somewhat different with the utterances of Origen. They come entirely from the period of his sojourn in Palestine, hence from the years *c*. 231 to *c*. 250 (Origen was born *c*. 185, died 253/4). When the attitudes he adopted to infant baptism are closely examined, it is clear that they all[1] stand on the defensive against the belief that infants do not need baptism, on the ground that as infants have not actually committed any sins, they do not require forgiveness of sins. This interpretation Origen combats with passages of Scripture that emphasize the inclusion of new-born children in the guilt of sin. But if the issue of infant baptism really did rest on a tradition handed down from the Apostles and universally recognized as such by a long standing observance, the polemic of Origen with all its detailed references to infant baptism would have been super-fluous. There must have been circles, and that not small and uninfluential, whose members held a different opinion as to the necessity of infant bap-tism and who correspondingly maintained a different practice, in that they abstained from baptizing infants. Hence arises Origen's appeal to the 'tradition of the Church received from the Apostles' (*traditio ecclesiae ab apostolis*), which was the strongest argument that he possessed. It seems to me that Jeremias has gone beyond all warrant when he reads out of Origen's statements the conclusion, 'His witness holds good for practically

---

[1] *In Lev. hom.* VIII: 'We may add to these considerations the question, Why should baptism be given to infants, as is the custom of the Church? seeing that if there were nothing in infants which required remission and pardon, the grace of baptism would seem superfluous.'

In Luc. hom. XIV: 'Infants were baptized "for the remission of sins": for what sins? or when did they sin? Perchance because "no one is clean from pollution"; but this pollution is taken away by the sacrament of baptism, and it is for this reason that infants are baptized.'

Comm. in Rom. V. 9: 'For what sin is this one pigeon offered? Can a newborn child have committed sin? Yes, even then it has sin, for which the sacrifice is commanded to be offered and from which even he who is but a day old is said not to be free. It is of this sin that David is supposed to have said that which we cited earlier, "In sin did my mother conceive me", for there is no mention in the history of any particular sin that his mother had committed. For this reason the Church received a tradition from the Apostles to give baptism to infants too.'

The two other passages adduced by Jeremias are quite uncertain. Of the one (*Hom. in Jos.* VIII, 32), Jeremias himself writes, 'There is an element of uncertainty in this proof, because *infans* could also be meant in a metaphorical sense.' The other (*Comm. in. Matt.*, the parable of the vineyard, Matt. 20.1 ff.) concerns 'another allegorical interpretation' in which infant baptism 'though not expressly mentioned is presupposed' (p. 65 n. 5) .It is therefore needless for us to cite them here .

the whole eastern Church of his time.'[1] The idea that 'he could not have referred to infant baptism in so unqualified a manner as "the custom of the church" (*ecclesiae observantia*) if in his journeys he had come upon deviations in practice within the sphere of the great Church',[2] ignores the mentality and methods of Church Fathers engaged in controversy, quite apart from the consideration that there is nothing in the text to indicate it.[3] And when Jeremias goes so far as to say that Origen could not have so so spoken 'unless he had known that at least his father and probably also his grandfather had been baptized as παιδία',[4] he is under the dominance of modern ideas. The father of Origen, Leonides, was a Christian; he died as a martyr in the persecution under Septimius Severus in AD 202. But whether he had been a Christian from his *youth* is not so much as hinted at in the sources, so far as my knowledge goes. Not a word stands in them about his grandfather; indeed our scanty information about the Church of Egypt largely begins with the time of Origen's birth. Only a romantic conception of the early Church could assert that the martyr death of his father presupposed a long standing as a Christian; new converts and catechumens[5] go as joyfully to martyrdom as those who have been in the membership of the Church for a long time. The most we can say is that Leonides had been a Christian for at any rate twelve years when he died, for he himself had instructed Origen in the Christian faith. If it be so wished, Leonides may be regarded as a Christian from his youth— although even to go as far as that is to forsake the foundation of the sources; but to affirm that both he and his father received baptism as infants is plainly not possible, even though such an admission has to give up the back-reference to 'the first half of that (second) century'.[6] There is no doubting that infant baptism took place between 230 and 250 in *Palestine* (or in parts of it) 'according to the custom of the Church'. It need not further be doubted that the usage in that place is older. But it seems to me that Origen's statements can be explained only on the assumption that this 'custom of the Church' in Palestine (and elsewhere) *is not yet very old*. For only on this presupposition is it explicable that the voices against infant baptism are still so strong that Origen has to enter into discussion

---

[1] p. 70.   [2] p. 70.

[3] It might have been expected that when Origen polemized against other interpretations he would have appealed not only to the *ab apostolis*, but to the fact that the Church everywhere maintained this custom.

[4] p. 66.

[5] The *Church Order* of Hippolytus assumes without argument that in the case of martyr death of catechumens, their blood baptism is a substitute for water baptism (44 [xix]).

[6] p. 66.

with them time and again. A beginning of this 'custom of the Church' about the end of the second century leaves enough time before AD 230/250 for the formation of a firm ecclesiastical usage, and on the other hand it explains why the arguments against it have not yet been silenced.[1]

The so-called *Church Order* of Hippolytus at first sight appears to be quite unambiguous. Here it declares (and the Coptic and Ethiopic texts agree almost exactly): 'First the little ones should be baptized. All who can speak for themselves should speak. For those however who cannot, their parents or another who belongs to their family should speak' (46.4 [xxi 4]).[2] Here it seems clear that along with children of maturer years the youngest also receive baptism. Although no indication is given as to whether this baptism is obligatory or only the rule, it is at least to be inferred from the text that it takes place often enough to demand an official regulation, and that this situation prevails at the beginning of the third century—presuming that the section really does go back to the time of Hippolytus (AD 235). For whereas the *Church Order* has come down to us in various translations, Sahidic, Bohairic, Ethiopic, Arabic, Latin, the original Greek text has almost entirely disappeared. The Sahidic tradition goes back to a manuscript of the year AD 1006, while the Bohairic, Ethiopic and Arabic manuscripts are even later. They all originate in a common textual tradition,[3] which quite certainly took its rise long after the death of Hippolytus.[4] The Latin tradition of the original Greek text can be put back into the end of the fourth century (the oldest manuscript comes from the period *c.* AD 500), but the extant fragments unfortunately do not contain the chapter on baptism. If we take into account that the texts immediately preceding the chapter on baptism deal exclusively with adult catechumens, notably with the (three-year) duration of the catechumenate (42 [xvii]), their participation in the worship (43 [xviii] and the martyrdom of catechumens (44 [xix]—their blood baptism replaces water baptism), then the affirmation is at least *possible* that the section relating to the baptism of children is an interpolation from a later age and has nothing to do with Hippolytus and the usage of his time. Immediately before this (45 [xx]) detailed instructions are given concerning the recipients of baptism: their life is to be examined, their behaviour during the period of

[1] It is *these* arguments that in reality correspond to a view that reaches back to Apostolic times.

[2] So in the Coptic text: Till/Leipoldt, p. 19; the Ethiopic text is quite similar: H. Duensing, *Der äthiopische Text der Kirchenordnung des Hippolyts* (Abh. der Göttinger Ak. d. Wiss. III, 32), Göttingen, 1946, p. 55.

[3] Their textual agreement therefore is no argument for the originality of their text.

[4] On this cf. G. Dix, *op. cit.*; J. M. Hanssens, *La Liturgie d'Hippolyte* (Orientalia Christiana Analecta 155), Rome, 1959.

D

catechumenate must be tested, witnesses for this are to be brought forward, on the Friday and Saturday before the baptism they should fast,[1]
and the night leading to Sunday should be spent together in the reading of
Scripture and in prayer till the baptism begins on the Sunday morning at
cock-crow with the prayer for the baptismal water. All that is clearly
designed for adults only, and in any case not for infants. And when we
observe that immediately after the text concerning the baptism of children
and infants (46.4 [xxi 4]) instructions for the baptism of men and women
follow (46.5 ff. [xxi 5 ff.]), all the needful material is present for a plausible
interpolation hypothesis which would date the insertion of the section on
the baptism of children many generations after Hippolytus. It could have
taken the place when the common text for the (oriental) translations was
freshly edited.

But we shall not uphold that view, if only because our case would
thereby be simplified. The *lectio difficilior* will unhesitatingly be accepted
as the right one. For if we find infant baptism in Africa *c.* 250 (Cyprian)
and its observance in Palestine *c.* 230/250 (Origen), why should it not
have existed in Rome, say *c.* 220 ? Yet one thing must be said quite plainly:
The conclusions for the early period of the Church that Jeremias tries to
draw from the *Church Order* of Hippolytus (as in the case of Origen) are
impossible (as also in Origen's case). Jeremias writes: 'It is true that the
Apostolic Tradition, as far as its composition goes, must be dated *c.* 215,
but its material is older, and it would actually be a mistake if we were to
reckon the work merely as evidence for the beginning of the third century.
For Hippolytus who probably incorporated the Church Order into his
book Περὶ χαρισμάτων ἀποστολικὴ παράδοσις as its second part, had no
intention of introducing new rules for church action, but as the title of his
work indicates, of setting down the older ("apostolic") tradition. And this
is true also of infant baptism.'[2] That is not so. For it is precisely *not* the
characteristic of a Church Order that it 'has no intention of introducing
new rules for church action, but . . . of setting down the older ("apostolic")
tradition.' The situation is just the reverse of this: a Church Order has the
intention of finally establishing the church situation of *its* time, or the per-
ceptions and demands of its author, by means of an appeal (which is
always made) back to the Apostolic age, and thus of securing for itself an
anchorage for all the time—until a new Church Order comes along and
sets the old one aside and tries to establish something which befits the new
time. This is the explanation of the perpetual appearance of new Church
Orders. Even when and where they do conserve and hand on the old texts,

---

[1] So Dix, xx 7; Till/Leipoldt 45.6 speak only of Friday.   [2] p. 74.

they enlarge them through fresh modifications. With respect to their intentions the Church Orders look not backwards but *forwards*. The author of the *Didache*, for instance, desires to solve the problems of *his* time and puts this solution in the mouth of the Apostles or of the Lord only because he hopes by this means to achieve attestation and validity. The same thing happens ever and again. Naturally whatever belongs to the old order and is useful for the new is permitted to remain, but the really important thing to the composer of a Church Order is always the *new*, otherwise he would not have needed to write it. Similarly it was precisely when infant baptism as a general Church custom was relatively new that it required a regulation and anchorage in the baptismal ritual, and this it has gained in the Church Order of Hippolytus. Assuming that the section on the baptism of children and infants really does stem from Hippolytus, his Church Order takes us no further back than Origen does, namely to the end of the second century. And the same applies also to Cyprian, as a consideration of the statements of Tertullian prove.[1] Here also we are able to observe how Tertullian sets himself in opposition to a development that had manifestly taken its beginning not long before—on grounds which can be more precisely given and which once more lead us to the outgoings of the second century.[2]

But something further must be said on the theme of 'missionary baptism'. Our earlier remarks[3] can be amplified by an example from the sources, viz. from the *Church Order* of Hippolytus.[4] To Jeremias it is quite obvious that a 'missionary baptism', such as is described in the *Church Order* of Hippolytus, essentially includes a whole family. The infants who receive the baptism thus belong to the parents, and together they all consummate their 'conversion' to the Church. It is not clear to me how the text of Hippolytus can be understood under these presuppositions. For according to his Church Order the children and infants are baptized first. After their baptism follows that of the adult men, and after that is completed the women are baptized. The various actions are carefully separated from each other, no doubt in part at least because the baptizands have laid aside their garments; a baptism by immersion is in view, which is received naked.[5] Now it is expressly said with regard to the youngest children, who cannot yet speak, that 'their parents . . . or another who belongs to their family' should answer the baptismal questions and render the baptismal confession. How can their parents—or other adherents of the family—do that, if they, as Jeremias maintains, come over *together* with their children

---

[1] On this see below, pp. 68 f.   [2] See below, pp. 103 f.   [3] See above, pp. 42 ff.
[4] We return yet again to this subject on p. 79.   [5] 46.10.

and on that account quite plainly are baptized only *after* their children? Only a full Christian is in a position to answer for others at baptism, as obtains even in baptismal prescriptions of today. In the case of these parents and relations therefore we have to do with *Christians*, hence these infants and children are children of Christian families. It is not possible to evade this, for example by saying, 'A member of the family who has already been converted to Christianity has to fulfil the function of the parents.' Jeremias has in view the simultaneous entry of 'houses' into the Church, thus of all who belong to a family; and moreover what purpose does the naming of the parents serve? It is not open to us to interpret the 'parents' of sponsors,[1] for the reference of the text to other members of the family (applicable to such occasions as when the parents are dead or ill?) must be only to physical parents. There is no alternative therefore but to interpret the infants as belonging to Christian parents; on that admission the theory of 'missionary baptism' once more falls apart. Undoubtedly catechumens are also present, but the children—at least the infants among them—come from Christian marriages. As for the older children, who have to be capable of acting independently in the far from simple rite of baptism and of answering for themselves, nothing lies nearer than to suppose that they also come from Christian families, at least in part. Where catechumens who are being baptized have little children, these latter are evidently kept over to the next baptism, or to a later one, except when they have fully initiated Christians among their relations who can assist at the baptism; but Jeremias' presumption that whole 'houses' enter the Church could certainly not be general. I do not see how the text of the *Church Order* of Hippolytus can be otherwise understood without resorting to complicated reinterpretations.

[1] In later centuries (cf. e.g. the report of the Egeria) we find '*patres*' and '*matres*' evidently so understood.

3

Patristic Statements concerning Infant Baptism from the Beginning to the End of the Second Century

OUR CONSIDERATION of the three texts was placed early in the discussion to get some firm ground beneath our feet. They all belong to the first half of the third century and they bear witness to the existence of infant baptism at that time. But what kind of witness does the preceding period yield? We are to consider the writers of the second century from the point of view of what can be gleaned from them of the existence or non-existence of infant baptism; first the Apostolic Fathers, then the Apologists who overlap them in time, then Irenaeus, and finally Clement of Alexandria, with whom we come almost exactly to the year 200 (the information about him emanating from the time after 202 is scanty and doubtful). Tertullian belongs to the end of the second century and will have to be considered in a special section, for his activity extends beyond the limits of the century (almost all his declarations on this theme belong to the later period) and on other grounds he requires separate treatment.

The Apostolic Fathers do not offer much material on our theme. Only three of the writings that make up this collection fall to be considered: the *Didache*, the *Shepherd of Hermas*, the *Letter of Barnabas*. What they do say appears to be so insignificant that Jeremias either does not discuss them (as the *Shepherd of Hermas*) or he only mentions them in other connections (so the *Didache* and the *Letter of Barnabas*). Nevertheless they seem to me to yield at least some hints, if not more, worthy of consideration. For example, the *Didache* deals with baptism in a special chapter (7). It is clear that certain baptismal instruction is given prior to the baptism of which it speaks, and the pattern for this teaching is laid down in chapters 1–6. The presupposition of baptismal instruction itself automatically rules out infants and little children. If the contents of this baptismal instruction be more closely examined it will be seen that both children and those who are growing up are excluded from it and that only the truly adult come into consideration as recipients of the instruction and of the baptism. In 7.4 it is further prescribed that the administrator and the receivers of baptism should fast beforehand—the candidates for one or two days; that likewise eliminates infants. It is to be assumed that after the baptism the celebration of the eucharist follows (according to 9.5 it should be administered only to the baptized); for that also infants do not come into consideration.

The *Shepherd of Hermas* seems to presuppose a period of probation prior to baptism (cf. Vis. III, 7.3); the affirmation that baptism cleanses only sins that have been committed beforehand[1] shows that Hermas also thinks of adults only as recipients of baptism, and in any case his terms do not have regard to infants. The same applies to the *Letter of Barnabas*, for he talks about Christians descending into the water of baptism 'full of sins and defilement of the flesh' (11.11).

The question of the date of these three writings is of importance. If we place them in the period from *c.* 100 to *c.* 150 and in the order *Didache*, *Letter of Barnabas*, *Shepherd of Hermas*, we stand in assured limits. The *Didache*, which many date before AD 100, stands at the beginning of this period, the *Shepherd of Hermas* at its end. In that case we find ourselves in the era of the latest writings of the New Testament. And at least the first author of the group of Apologists shortly to be considered, Aristides, belongs to the same period of time, for according to Eusebius he wrote in the time of the Emperor Hadrian, AD 117–138. Possibly the same applies to Justin, who was martyred *c.* AD 165; his *Apology* was written during the reign of Antoninus Pius, who ruled 138–161. In this manner a close chain of witnesses is gained, reaching right back into the sub-apostolic age.

We turn our attention at once to Justin, since he can be quickly dismissed (Aristides requires a more thorough discussion). From Justin, to whom allusion has already been made,[2] we have a detailed description of baptism, in the so-called *First Apology*, chapter 61. It, too, probably presupposes adults exclusively, but certainly not infants. Only they are permitted to be baptized who are convinced of the truth of the Christian teaching and who undertake to lead a life in accordance with it ('All who are persuaded and believe that the things taught and declared by us are true, and who promise that they can live accordingly are instructed. . . .').[3] Candidates for baptism seek with fasting forgiveness from God for the sins they have earlier committed.[4] They are then led to the water[5] and after-

---

[1] Mand. IV, 3.1–2.   [2] See above, p. 43.
[3] 61.2 f.: ὅσοι ἄν πεισθῶσι καὶ πιστεύωσιν ἀληθῆ ταῦτα τὰ ὑφ' ἡμῶν διδασκόμενα καὶ λεγόμενα εἶναι, καὶ βιοῦν οὕτως δύνασθαι ὑπισχνῶνται.   [4] *Ibid.*   [5] 61.3.

wards to the gathering of the believers,[1] where after prayer,[2] the giving and receiving of the kiss of brotherhood,[3] and offering of the elements and the thanksgiving,[4] they finally receive the eucharist in bread, wine and water.[5] All these features make the presupposition of a participation of infants in the baptismal event appear unthinkable.

The *Apology* of Aristides[6] is the first of the writings we are dealing with in this section to which Jeremias has given detailed consideration. He finds in 15.11 an allusion to baptism. Admittedly the sacraments are not directly mentioned, nevertheless, he contends, it is necessary rightly to understand the passage: 'And when a child (τέκνον) is born to them they thank God; and if it die in infancy (νήπιον) they thank him exceedingly, because it departed this life sinless.'[7] In Jeremias' view 15.11 is to be set alongside the parallel in 17.4, 'where the writer says, "And if it happens that one of them (the pagans) is converted, he is ashamed before the Christians of the things that he has done, and thanks God, saying 'In ignorance have I done them'. And he purifies his heart, and his sins are forgiven him." In this passage the focal expression "to thank God" is a reference to baptism.'[8] The point of interest therefore is the εὐχαριστοῦσιν of 15.11 and the 'thank God' of 17.4 (the Greek text is not preserved here). Nevertheless it appears to me that such an interpretation goes beyond what is legitimate in both places.

Jeremias himself alludes to the fact that the expression 'to thank God' is frequently met with in Aristides ('Aristides loves this expression'[9]), and calls attention to his use of it to describe prayers in the morning and grace at meals (15.10) as also for the service at the death of a church member (15.11). These passages are extant in the Greek text, which at 15.10 reads εὐχαριστοῦντες αὐτῷ (in the Barlaam-Josaphat Text[10]) or εὐχαριστοῦσιν αὐτῷ (so in Pap. B.M. 2486[11]) κατὰ πρωΐας καὶ πᾶσαν ὥραν ἐν παντὶ βρωτῷ (=βρωτῷ or βρώματι in Barl. Joas.) καὶ ποτῷ. Finally 15.11 says, 'And when a righteous man among them departs from this world, they rejoice and thank God and accompany his body, as if he were journeying from one place to another.'[12] The passage about the birth and death of a child

[1] 65.1.   [2] *Ibid.*   [3] 65.2.   [4] 65.3.   [5] 65.5.
[6] It has come down to us really in the Syriac alone; a few parts of the original Greek text have been preserved in some papyrus fragments and in the indirect tradition of the Barlaam-Josaphat romance.
[7] Jeremias, p. 71.   [8] *Ibid.*   [9] *Ibid.*
[10] R. Seeberg, *Der Apologet Aristides, der Text seiner uns erhalten Schriften*, 1894, p. 58; E. J. Goodspeed, *Die ältesten Apologeten*, 1914, p. 21; J. R. Harris and J. A. Robinson, *The Apology of Aristides* (Texts and Studies, I, 1), Cambridge, 1891, p. 111.
[11] H. J. M. Milne, 'A New Fragment of the Apology of Aristides', *JTS* 25 (1924), p. 76.
[12] In Pap. B.M. 2486 the text reads: ἐὰν δὲ καὶ ἀποθάνῃ τις εὐσεβὴς ἐξ αὐτῶν χαίρουσιν καὶ εὐχαριστοῦσιν καὶ προσεύχονται περὶ αὐτοῦ καὶ προπέμπουσιν ὡς ἀποδημοῦντα.

follows on immediately, 'And when a child is born to one of them they praise God, and if again it should happen that it dies in its childhood they praise God mightily, because it has gone through the world without sin.'[1] The significance of this becomes clear as the whole train of thought is taken into account. 'And when again they see that one of their number has died in his godlessness or in his sins, then they weep over him bitterly and sigh, as for one who is at the point of going to his punishment.'[2] In my judgment one simply cannot say, as Jeremias does, 'The special hymn of praise to God which the congregation raises at the burial of a little child "because it departed this life 'sinless' " (ἀναμάρτητον, 15.11) can hardly refer to the innocence of childhood, but much more probably to the forgiveness which is given in baptism.'[3] On the contrary the deduction must be drawn that here a real sinlessness of the child is presupposed[4] in contrast to the sinfulness of the Christian[5] who, despite his baptism(!) does not die in his advanced age in the purity demanded of Christians. The whole passage speaks of those who belong to the Church and makes a contrast between purity and impurity in order to show the high standard of the moral demands of Christians. It appears to me that the εὐχαριστοῦσιν in 15.11 concerning the birth of the child cannot be referred to baptism on account of the following ὑπερευχαριστοῦσιν; if εὐχαριστοῦσιν is to be understood as meaning baptize, what does ὑπερευχαριστοῦσιν signify, occurring only six words later? Moreover the parallelism with the other places plainly encourages the interpretation, 'thank God (in prayer)'. Similarly 17.4 gives no justification for relating the 'thank God' to baptism. The first sentence, 'If it happens that one of them is converted, he is ashamed before the Christians of the things that he has done, and he thanks God and says, "In ignorance have I done this",'[6] signifies no more than that the convert thanks God for his conversion. If there is any reflection of baptism it occurs in the *following* sentence: 'He cleanses his heart (i.e. submits to baptism—or is confession of sins alone meant?) and his sins are (therein!) forgiven him.'[7]

---

[1] The text cited by Milne reads somewhat differently:

ἐπὰν δὲ τέκνον γεννηθῇ αὐτοῖς εὐχαριστοῦσιν τῷ θεῷ ἐὰν δὲ νήπιον <ἐ>ξέλθῃ ὑπερευχαριστοῦσιν ὅτι ἀναμάρτητον ἀπῆλθεν.

[2] In the text of Milne, ἐὰν δὲ ἁμαρτίας τις ἔχων ἀποθάνῃ κλαίουσιν ὡς ἐπὶ κόλασιν ἀπερχομένου αὐτοῦ.

[3] p. 71.

[4] An idea which meets us elsewhere, cf. the contemporary *Hermas*, Sim. IX, 31.3; Athenagoras, *De res mort.* 14, etc.; on this see below, pp. 104 f.

[5] The Syriac text unambiguously represents this meaning; cf. also Harris and Robinson, p. 50: 'that one of their number has died in his iniquity'.

[6] Seeberg, p. 61; Goodspeed, p. 23; Harris and Robinson, p. 51.

[7] So also C. Vona, 'L'Apologia di Aristide', *Lateranum* N.S. XVI, 1–4, Rome, 1950, pp. 41 f. He finds a mention of baptism only in 17.4 but in none of the other passages.

Another passage in the *Apology* of Aristides, 15.6, astonishingly finds no mention in Jeremias' work, yet it is deeply significant and important for our theme, for it appears to me really to speak of baptism, indeed of the baptism of children; but it is 'children's baptism' (*Kindertaufe*) in the right sense, because the children are not infants but are baptized at a more advanced age. Moreover the passage speaks unequivocally of the children of Christians, hence not of 'missionary baptism' to which Jeremias accords a higher age. In 15.6 it is related, 'Now they instruct the servants and maids or the children, when any of them have such, that they become Christians, on account of the love which they have for them. And when they have become Christians they call them brothers without distinction.'[1] This passage is extraordinarily instructive. First, to make the interpretation of the Syriac text quite sure: the passage speaks of *Christians*; servants, maidservants, children are ranged alongside one another and to them the term 'Christians' relates—it cannot be so translated as if it referred to children of the maidservants and servants! This interpretation is the one generally adopted; Seeberg,[2] Hennecke,[3] and Harris and Robinson[4] all render it in this way. Fortunately the Greek form of the text (or at least a form) is preserved for us in the Papyrus 2486 of the British Museum:

ἀλλὰ καὶ δούλους καὶ παιδίσκας ἐὰν ἔχωσιν ἢ τέκνα πείθουσιν αὐτοὺς χρειστιανοὺς γενέσθαι ἵνα ἔχωσιν εὐνόους καὶ ὅταν γένωνται τοιοῦτοι ἀδελφοὺς καλοῦσιν αὐτοὺς ἀμέριστοι ὄντες.[5] This text also makes it impossible to understand the τέκνα as children of the servants. According to Aristides, then, a baptism of these children while still infants is excluded, even though they come from Christian families (newly converted Christians are not here in view!). The impression is given that they are baptized only after they have attained the needful insight, hence not before they have become several years old. Then they are baptized and, despite their youth, are regarded as full Christians, and they participate in the eucharist (a custom which is also attested by Cyprian in the third century). Another feature of importance emerges if the interpretation of the Syriac text is correct (it diverges somewhat from the Greek at this point):[6] it hints of a

---

[1] Seeberg, p. 57; Goodspeed, p. 20; Harris and Robinson, p. 49.

[2] As in 1894, so also in 1893, R. Seeberg, *Die Apologie des Aristides untersucht und wiederhergestellt* (Forschungen zur Geschichte des neutestamentlichen Kanons V, 2, ed. T. Zahn), p. 398; cf. also *Neue Kirchliche Zeitschrift*, II (1893), p. 961.

[3] *Die Apologie des Aristides* (TU, IV, 3) (1893), p. 37.

[4] *The Apology of Aristides* (Texts and Studies, I, 1, 1893), p. 49: 'But as for *their* servants or handmaids, or *their* children if any of them have any, they persuade them to become Christians for the love that they have towards them; and when they become so, they call them without distinction brethren.'   [5] Milne, p. 74.

[6] The Greek e.g. possibly (and rightly?) relates the ἐὰν ἔχωσιν only to the servants and maidservants.

condition of affairs that must occupy our attention later,[1] namely that the number of children born in Christian marriages at the time of Aristides, i.e. in the first decades of the second century, is not particularly large; as with the possession of servants, they are reckoned only as a possibility, not as the rule.

In Aristides' *Apology* (15.6) we appear to have a piece of evidence that not only indirectly excludes infant baptism, as the previous patristic testimonies, but that expressly postpones the baptism even of the children of Christian parents to a later age. The baptism follows after the children have received instruction in Christian teaching.

This brings us to Irenaeus, who in time follows on Justin (Irenaeus became Bishop of Lyons 177/8 and so was born *c.* AD 140–150). Jeremias follows Windisch[2] when he claims Irenaeus as a witness for infant baptism. But in my view their interpretation takes account only of the first part of what Irenaeus said in his work *Against Heresies*, II, 22.4:[3] 'For he came to save all through means of himself—all, I say, who through him are born again to God (*renascuntur in Deum*)—infants, and children, and boys, and youths, and old men.' If the text is broken off at this point it is possible to conclude with Jeremias, 'Since Irenaeus, following the fully established and quite unvarying terminology of the Church, describes baptism as "regeneration unto God" (*regeneratio in Deum*), he bears witness in our passage to infant baptism and presupposes it as "an unquestioned practice of the Church".'[4] But if the context of Irenaeus' statement be taken into account, including that which precedes as well as that which follows, the conclusion is by no means so certain. Irenaeus has just said that Jesus was thirty years old when he was baptized. After that event he came to Jerusalem at an age that befitted a teacher, 'that he might be properly acknowledged by all as a teacher . . . not despising or evading any condition of humanity, nor setting aside in himself that law which he had appointed for the human race, but *sanctifying every age by that period corresponding to it which belonged to himself.*' Jeremias' basic text follows and Irenaeus continues without a break: '*He therefore passed through every age, becoming an infant for infants, thus sanctifying infants, a child for children, thus sanctifying those who are of this age, being at the same time made to them an example of piety, righteousness, and submission*; a youth for youths,

---

[1] See below, p. 102 f.   [2] *ZNW* 28, 1929, p. 135.

[3] Translator's note: This is the enumeration in Stieren, p. 358 (reproduced in MPG 7.783 f.). In his text the author adopts that given by Harvey, I, 330 and Kraft, nr. 10, p. 10, viz. II, 23.2. Instead of reproducing the extensive citations from Irenaeus in the Latin, as the author has done, I have employed the English rendering of A. Roberts and J. Donaldson in *The Ante-Nicene Fathers*, I (1887), p. 391.

[4] p. 73. The citation in the last clause comes from Windisch, p. 135.

becoming an example to youths, and thus sanctifying them for the Lord. So likewise he was an old man for old men, that he might be a perfect teacher for all, not merely as respects the setting forth of the truth, but also as regards age, sanctifying at the same time the aged also, and becoming an example to them likewise. Then at last, he came on to death itself, that he might be "the first born from the dead, that in all things he might have the pre-eminence", the Prince of life, existing before all, and going before all.' It does not seem apparent to me that Irenaeus has baptism in view here, and certainly there is no thought of infant baptism; he is concerned solely with the fact that Jesus sanctified all humanity in that he was made like all, lived through all ages of life and was an example to all ('not merely as respects the setting forth of the truth, but also as regards age'!). Nothing more than this is presupposed; nothing more than this is stated; therefore nothing more than this should be sought from it.

Lastly Clement of Alexandria is accorded a very brief treatment by Jeremias. 'We shall do well to disregard Clement of Alexandria,' he writes.[1] For in his 'allegorical figure of the children who are drawn from the water (by the fisher)[2] . . . it is indeed possible that he is thinking of the baptism of children, but he might be thinking of children in the faith (cf. I Peter 2.1 f.) whom the missionary brings to baptism';[3] the second alternative without doubt is the correct one. Yet I do not think that we should be satisfied with a conclusion of this kind. Apart from the fact that a far larger number of passages relating to baptism occur in his writings than appears from Jeremias,[4] in my judgment a deduction can be drawn from Clement of no small significance for our investigation. Out of the more than twenty passages listed by Stählin in his index (among which those relating to παῖς, νήπιος, etc., must be reckoned) the conclusion seems clear to me that the baptism of children falls outside the range of Clement's view (to choose a cautious mode of expression); i.e. either it is without significance for *him*, or it does not exist for his time. In the very passage where Clement adduces some detailed considerations that touch upon our theme, and where all the *loci classici* appear which, according to Jeremias, signify the crystallization points of the view of child baptism in early times, Clement does not so much as breathe a word on the subject. For example in *Paedagogos*, I, 5, which bears the significant superscription: 'All who concern themselves with the truth are children of God' (οἱ πάντες οἱ περὶ τὴν ἀλήθειαν καταγινόμενοι παῖδες παρὰ τῷ θεῷ), a long row of passages

---

[1] p. 64. [2] *Paedagogos* III, 17, § 59.2. [3] pp. 64 f.
[4] More also than Kraft adduces (no. 11, pp. 10 f.), cf. the detailed index of Stählin in vol. 4 of his edition in the GCS under Βάπτισμα, p. 293.

relating to children are adduced and expounded, including the *pericope* about the blessing of the children by Jesus. Yet nowhere is a verbal interpretation of these 'children' to be found, but they are always regarded as adult Christians. That occurs even where one might inevitably expect such a reference, e.g. when Matt. 21.16 is quoted with the citation from Ps. 8.3, 'Out of the mouth of infants and sucklings thou has perfected praise.'[1] In this chapter more than a page is devoted to the exposition of the word νήπιος, infant,[2] yet nowhere is a reference to real children to be found and none to their baptism. Chapter 6 develops this reflection: 'To those who take the name of children and infants the teaching of the first disciples is revealed.'[3] In this connection baptism is discussed in §§26.1–3; 30.1–32.1, again without any reference to the baptism of real children. In §§39–42, 48 f., there is a meditation that takes into account the physical events of birth and the nourishment of children, but always in such a way that everything is related to grown believers, never in such a manner that a practice of the baptism of children or of infants remotely comes into view. The Logos is even viewed as exclusively the 'instructor of men and women' (ἀνδρῶν καὶ γυναικῶν παιδαγωγός, the superscription to chapter 4). Baptism is for the forgiveness of faults which have actually been committed to this point of time (see the whole of chapter 24 in Book IV of the *Stromateis*); it is 'the repentance of a one-time unbeliever' (ἡ τοῦ ποτὲ ἀπίστου μετάνοια) therefore it has no place for children or infants, for 'the foundation of redemption is the faith that proceeds from a man's volition' (θεμέλιος τῆς σωτηρίας ἑκούσιος πίστις).[4]

---

[1] § 12.5 ff. (GCS, p. 97).   [2] §§ 19 f. (GCS, pp. 101 f.).

[3] πρὸς τοὺς ὑπολαμβάνοντας τὴν τῶν παιδίων καὶ νηπίων προσηγορίαν τὴν τῶν πρώτων μαθημάτων αἰνίττεσθαι διδαχήν, GCS, p. 104.

[4] *Strom* II, 3, § 11.2 (GCS, p. 119).

4

Tertullian

WE COME now to Tertullian, i.e. to the turn of the second and third centuries AD, the period immediately preceding that which we considered in chapter 2. Tertullian was born c. 160 and died after 220; Hippolytus, Origen and Cyprian followed immediately after, so in considering him the chain of patristic testimonies and their investigation to the middle of the third century is complete.

In itself Tertullian's position is quite clear. He devoted a whole volume to the question of baptism (*De baptismo*). His appeal in opposition to the baptism of infants and young children is well known: 'Why does the age of innocence hasten to the remission of sins?'[1] The situation presupposed seems plain enough: in Carthage a significant tendency to baptize infants or young children is evidently in motion, but Tertullian expressly opposes it. He voices his opinion with all clarity just before the sentence quoted above: 'Let them "come" therefore when they grow older; let them "come" when they are able to learn, when they can be instructed whither they should "come"; let them become Christians when they can know Christ.'[2] Tertullian therefore holds that it is right to baptize children only when they have reached an age when an understanding of Christianity and a confession of Christ on their own part is possible. All this springs from his interpretation of the dominical saying in Matt. 19.14, 'Do not forbid them to come to me,' which he sets at the head of the discussion. His viewpoint is part and parcel of a broader context which stands under the unexpressed superscription, 'The postponement of baptism is preferable.'[3] Accordingly unmarried women, especially virgins but also widows, are advised to postpone baptism, since they are endangered by reason of temptation which they might not be able to withstand.[4] Tertullian's

[1] *Quid festinat innocens aetas ad remissionem peccatorum? De baptismo* 18.5 (CC 1, p. 293); Kraft no. 13b, p. 14.
[2] *Veniant ergo dum adolescunt, dum discunt, dum quo veniant docentur; fiant Christiani, cum Christum nosse potuerint (ibid).*
[3] *Cunctatio baptismi utilior est, de bapt.* 18.4 (CC 1, p. 293).   [4] *De bapt.* 18.6.

grounds for the necessity of postponing baptism do not sound exactly convincing: sponsors expose themselves to needless danger through infant baptism, for they may either be hindered by their own death from carrying out the promise which they make for the baptized in a representative capacity, or the baptized themselves may develop in a manner different from that which is hoped for in baptism. One can observe in this rather tortuous argumentation how Tertullian endeavours by every means in his power to stem the tide of development towards infant baptism. Nevertheless there is no doubting his emphatic opposition to this movement, and in face of the increasingly weighty moral position he enjoyed in the church of Carthage at that time, it had no little significance and effect. It certainly influenced many and perhaps delayed the development of infant baptism in some circles.

Jeremias endeavours to minimize this position of Tertullian by relegating the volume under discussion to a lower category and characterizing it as an 'occasional writing'.[1] That is out of the question, for *all* the writings of Tertullian, with but few exceptions (e.g. *De anima*), were composed to meet particular situations. Tertullian is not a systematic author who fashions his literary work in accordance with a previously established plan, carefully expanding his position in all directions; rather he takes up his pen on definite occasions to deal with live issues according to the needs of the moment. Further, Jeremias explains that *De baptismo* apparently 'had its origin in addresses to Carthaginian catechumens and neophytes', and therefore 'in the whole tract Tertullian has the baptism of converts primarily in view'.[2] This category is not suitable to Tertullian's writing. For one thing he does not speak to catechumens only; he expressly declares that *De baptismo* was written also in order to strengthen full members of the Church against heretical teaching, 'instructing not only such as are just becoming formed in the faith'.[3] It is Tertullian's intention to address the *entire* Church, among which of course the catechumens are to be numbered, some of them having belonged to it for years. Moreover among those brought to baptism, or potentially coming into consideration for it, a not inconsiderable group of children, both younger and older, must have been involved, otherwise Tertullian would not have accorded them special treatment. Nor would Tertullian have been compelled to embark on a discussion solely in connection with the children of catechu-

---

[1] p. 82.   [2] *Ibid.*

[3] *Instruens tam eos qui cum maxime formantur, De bapt.* 1.1 (CC 1, p. 277). Cf. the reference in 20.5, 'blessed ones whom the grace of God awaits' (*benedicti quos gratia dei expectat*) (CC 1, p. 295). The same also applies to the other writings to be adduced, *De spectaculis* (cf. 1.1) and *De paenitentia* (cf. 6.14, etc.).

mens; the question as to the right age for baptism was posed because of
the presence of newly-born children in the Christian community. Tertullian's expositions in *De baptismo* appear to presuppose a situation
parallel to that in the *Church Order* of Hippolytus; an unprejudiced reading of his book does not yield the impression that *De baptismo* speaks only
of the children of pagans;[1] rather the impression is repeatedly given that
Tertullian speaks of *all* children or infants in the community, irrespective
of whether they belong to parents already baptized or to catechumens.

Finally, it must be pointed out that Jeremias gives detailed consideration
only to *De baptismo* and *De anima* (even *De paenitentia* receives but passing
notice from him). Yet we possess two further writings in which Tertullian
expresses his views on baptism: *De spectaculis* and *De corona*. A complete
picture can be gained only when consideration is taken of them. It is
important to observe the chronological sequence of these works. In their
relative chronological order[2] they appear thus:

> *De spectaculis* ⎫
> *De baptismo*   ⎬ pre-Montanist
> *De paenitentia* ⎭
>
> *De anima* ⎫
> *De corona* ⎬ Montanist

In relation to absolute chronology, surer statements beyond assigning
them to the pre-Montanist or Montanist periods are hardly possible; the
one relatively firm date is that of Tertullian's conversion to Montanism,
which is generally set in the year 207. The writings group themselves
around this date, but the temporal distance between the individual works
of the two groups could consist of a few years at most in some cases, while
others are possibly even contemporary (as perhaps *De anima* and *De
corona*).

One thing seems immediately clear: in his first as in his latest writings
Tertullian had in view the baptism of adults or of those who had recently
come to mature years, not the baptism of infants. *De spect.* 4 discusses the
baptismal confession, which Tertullian apprehends as renouncing the
devil and all his powers, including the forsaking of theatre performances

---

[1] This term itself is ambiguous and shows that we find ourselves in a situation to which
the views of Jeremias, taken over from the circumstances of earlier times, no longer fit;
in this case children of *catechumens* are in view.

[2] On this matter, cf. the chronological table in vol. 2 of the Corpus Christianorum,
pp. 1627 f., similarly Harnack, *Geschichte der altchristlichen Literatur bis Eusebius*[2], ed.
Aland, 1958, II, 2, pp. 295 f., who is in substantial agreement and only places *De corona*
(211) before *De anima*. For practical purposes they may both be viewed as roughly contemporary.

that are bound up with idolatry (see further chapter 24). The confession is made 'with our mouth',[1] a feature which effectively prevents its inclusion in infant baptism. In *De corona* 3 Tertullian describes the course of a baptism. In the rite, although before its actual administration, the believers abjure the devil and his pomp and his angels.[2] After the threefold immersion of baptism the newly baptized taste a mixture of milk and honey;[3] that could apply to infants also, but Tertullian continues: 'from that day we refrain from the daily bath for a whole week,'[4] something which surely does not have infants in view. The statements in *De baptismo* therefore do not stand in isolation, contrary to the impression given by Jeremias; Tertullian has not in his later writings modified the views represented in his work, nor has he 'dropped them altogether';[5] so far as anything can be concluded from his treatment of baptism in the works that fall to be considered, he has steadfastly maintained the same position. The earlier period of his writing as the later gives no indication that he was moving towards a justification or even a commendation of infant baptism.

What is the position, however, with the views expounded by Tertullian in *De anima* and *De paenitentia*? Does Jeremias believe he can here find support for his opinion that *De baptismo* represents a peculiar case? Let us begin with Tertullian's book *De anima*. From the arguments adduced by Tertullian in chapters 39–40 Jeremias draws the conclusion: 'Tertullian here not only presupposes the practice of infant baptism, he advocates it.'[6] In my judgment it ought to be pointed out at once that this passage of Tertullian's forms part of a basic treatise concerning the soul. In chapter 39[7] Tertullian first of all speaks of the gifts which are added to the soul from birth (immortality, rationality, sensibility, intelligence, freedom of the will).[8] From the beginning they are an object of envy to the devil. He darkens and perverts them, that they should not further be developed or used in the right way (39.1). The pagan customs practised at birth, described by Tertullian in detail in 39.2, actually give him an invitation to do so. When Tertullian asks in 39.2: 'Does anyone fail to devote to idolatrous service the entire head of his son, or to take out a hair or to shave off the whole with a razor, or to bind it up for an offering, or seal it for sacred use—in behalf of the clan, or the ancestry, for

---

[1] *Ore nostro*, *De spect.* 4.1 (CC 1, p. 231).
[2] *De cor.* 3.2 (CC 2, p. 1042). Tertullian uses here exactly the same words as in *De spect.* 4.
[3] *Lactis et mellis concordiam*, *De cor.* 3.3 (CC 2, pp. 1042 f.).
[4] *Exque eo die lauacro quotidiano per totam ebdomadem abstinemus.*
[5] p. 85.
[6] pp. 84 f.
[7] It is necessary to begin at 39.1—indeed actually at ch. 38—and not simply at 39.3 as Jeremias does, if a full understanding of the text is to be gained.
[8] *Immortalitas, rationalitas, sensualitas, intellectualitas, libertas arbitrii*, 38.6.

public or private devotion?'[1] it is clear that pagan children are in mind,[2] not all children, including the Christian. The last sentence of 39.3, with which Jeremias begins, *adeo nulla ferme nativitas munda est, utique ethnicorum*, in my view is falsely rendered when we translate it as he does: 'Therefore (since in every man by nature or because of pagan practices at birth there is a "demonic spirit") practically no birth is pure, especially in the case of pagans';[3] rather it should be rendered as Waszink does in his commentary: 'Practically nobody is completely pure at birth, i.e. among pagans.' What Tertullian says here relates to the heathen; this conclusion is reinforced when the preceding context is taken into account.

From this point Tertullian passes over at 39.4 to children of Christian marriages or to children of mixed marriages, and he does so by citing I Cor. 7.4; and while this gives the impression of being unmediated, in reality it is logical. Pagan children are almost all unclean from birth, but Christian children (or children of a marriage where one of the parents is Christian) are not so; he continues: 'It was because of this that the Apostle said, that when either of the parents was sanctified, the children were holy; and this is as much by the prerogative of the (Christian) seed as by the discipline of the institution.'[4] If the last sentence of 39.3 related to Christian children, this conclusion would not be possible (i.e. the inclusion of *hinc*, 'because of this', and the statement of the grounds for it). They are to be regarded as *sancti* 'when either of the parents was sanctified'; and in truth they are actually *born* as such! Thus far Tertullian simply inserts Paul's teaching into his own thought, but then with a direct citation of I Cor. 7.14 he gives an interpretation of Paul's view, to return once more to his general line. He comments, 'As if he meant us to understand that the children of believers were marked out for holiness, and therewith for salvation,'[5] for the protection of (mixed) marriages, which this was intended to maintain. 'Besides, he had not forgotten,' concludes Tertullian, 'what the Lord has so definitively stated,' and he then cites John 3.5; i.e. this presupposition of birth in holiness does not apply outside Christian

---

[1] *Quis non exinde aut totum filii caput reatui vovet aut aliquem excipit crinem aut totum novacula prosecat aut sacrificio obligat aut sacro obsignat, pro gentica, pro avita, pro publica aut privata devotione?* pp. 55 f., cited according to the edition of Waszink, Amsterdam, 1949, for the sake of the important commentary provided for this edition.

[2] The following sentence concerning Socrates, 'While yet a boy he was found by the spirit of the demon' (*puerum adhuc spiritus daemonicus invenit*), underscores this fact; similarly the assertion, 'Thus, too, it is that to all persons their genii are assigned' (*sic et omnibus genii deputantur*), clearly is not intended to apply to children of Christians.

[3] p. 84.

[4] *Hinc enim et apostolus ex sanctificato alterutro sexu sanctos procreari ait, tam ex seminis praerogativa quam ex institutionis disciplina*, Waszink, p. 56.

[5] *Quasi designatos tamen sanctitatis ac per hoc etiam salutis intelligi volens fidelium filios.*

E

marriages. At 40.1 accordingly, Tertullian is able to take up again his original train of argument, that there is virtually no pure birth; the excursus on children of Christian marriages is finished, the conclusion of 39.4 gave him the transition. Hence he can continue: 'Every soul, then, by reason of its birth, is enrolled in Adam until it is enrolled again in Christ; moreover, it is unclean all the while that it remains without this new enrolment; and because unclean, it is sinful and responsible also for the stain of the flesh with which it is united.'[1] The interpretation offered by Jeremias, quite apart from the fact that it begins too late and therefore does not interpret exactly the last sentence of 39.3, seems to me to miss the mark at its decisive point. Jeremias concludes from the text: 'Of them (the children of believers) he says that by their birth they are "marked out for holiness and therewith for salvation"; they are however, according to John 3.5 only made holy by baptism (39.4).'[2] In my judgment that is neither consistent with what Tertullian says nor does it correspond with his intention. Rather I would urge that Tertullian remains wholly on the lines of the viewpoint he has expressed elsewhere. To him it is self-evident that a man is unclean and in need of the cleansing of repentance and baptism; only the enrolment in the 'register of Christ' makes him free from sin. When born a pagan, this sin clings to a man in consequence of the snares of Satan that are set from birth on, and in particular pagan superstition almost automatically makes him the prey of the devil (exceptions are naturally conceivable!). Where a man has Christian parents, or even only one, this danger does not exist, for he is born as *sanctus*. Yet even here this original sanctity does not remain for ever; in a way it is only a firstfruits, for even the child born of Christians falls into sin. It is indeed originally *sanctus* (so far Tertullian follows Paul), but it is not yet completely so, for actually it is only *sanctus designatus*, marked out for holiness (so Tertullian circumscribes it), and this 'by the prerogative of the (Christian) seed' as also 'by the discipline of the institution'.[3] The child born of a Christian marriage also needs baptism, when through the course of the years it has become defiled by sin and has attained to the requisite knowledge ('responsible also for the stain of the flesh with which it is united').

---

[1] *Ita omnis anima, eo usque in Adam censetur, donec in Christo recenseatur, tamdiu immunda, quamdiu recenseatur; peccatrix autem, quia immunda, recipiens ignominiam et carnis ex societate*, 40.1.   [2] p. 84.

[3] *Ex institutionis disciplina*: Jeremias translates, 'because of their future education in Christian doctrine', p. 84. According to Jeremias, then, are we to understand that the order is first baptism, then instruction? In Tertullian's understanding this is excluded (cf. *De baptismo*, etc.): the order must be first instruction, then baptism! The child born of a Christian marriage is *sanctus designatus* because inevitably Christian instruction lies ahead of him, which, with its conclusion in baptism, will make him *sanctus*. This is yet another hint that *De anima* is to be interpreted otherwise than Jeremias does it.

In *De anima* 38.1 Tertullian is even able to say when this sinfulness begins: 'We maintain that the puberty of the soul coincides with that of the body,' and this is reached 'at about the fourteenth year of life';[1] 'and,' he observes, '*it drives man out of the paradise of innocence.*'[2] That surely means that the child born of Christians is clean to that point of time, since unlike the children of pagans he is not from his birth onwards given over to Satan, whether directly or indirectly.[3]

And further: what are we to make of the contradiction that Jeremias has discovered between the delaying of the baptism of infants and little children on the one hand, with which agrees the advice given to the unmarried, particularly virgins and widows, that they should postpone their baptism (in *De baptismo*), and on the other hand the polemic against the 'tendency to postpone joining the Church, because of the belief that in view of the forgiveness expected in baptism one could continue in sin until baptism without worrying', in *De paenitentia*? A right attitude to this requires a closer consideration of chapter 6.3–24, the section of *De paenitentia* that affords the basis for Jeremias' interpretation. On examination it will be found that Tertullian directs his polemic not against a postponement of *baptism*, but against a postponement of the *repentance* that precedes baptism. So far as I can see Tertullian does not say a word about postponing baptism. The catechumens against whom he inveighs are characterized by the following attitude, placed on the lips of one of them: 'But let us defer for a while the reality of our *repentance*; it will, I fancy, be time enough to be free from fault when we are absolved (i.e. in baptism!).'[4] Jeremias has been able to reach his conclusion only because he apparently interchanged repentance and baptism. Yet that repentance and baptism must be distinguished from one another is stated with all clarity in the first sentence of 6.3: 'A presumptuous confidence in baptism introduces all kinds of vicious delay and unprincipled fickleness with regard to

---

[1] *Pubertatem quoque animalem cum carnali dicimus convenire . . . a quarto decimo fere anno*, Waszink, p. 54. [2] *Et hominem de paradiso integritatis educit*, 38.2.

[3] Naturally the text remains extraordinarily difficult, and it should be explicitly stated that the manner of our description of the Christian child to the time of its later baptism is not stated by Tertullian in these express words. Nevertheless I think that such an interpretation, or one similar to it, does result from the totality of Tertullian's statements. In any case Jerome seems to me to have understood Tertullian rightly (Waszink, who dissents from the above interpretation in a few particulars, says that his utterance is 'the best commentary on this passage', p. 446): 'Your second problem was discussed by Tertullian in his book on monogamy (= *De anima*), asserting that the children of saints are said to be holy, because they are as candidates of the faith and not defiled by any of the filth of idolatry' (*ep.* 85.5; CSEL 55.137). At least the last sentence of *De anima* 39.3 has escaped the understanding of Jeremias but the interpretation adduced above is underscored.

[4] *Sed differamus tantisper paenitentiae veritatem; tunc opinor emandatos liquebit cum, absolvimur, De paen.* 6.6 (CC 1, p. 330).

repentance.'[1] That is, because forgiveness of sins (in baptism!) is in any case assured, the time that precedes baptism is used for evil doing instead of being 'a time for learning not to sin'.[2] 'Moreover, how foolish, how perverse,' exclaims Tertullian, 'to expect pardon of sins (i.e. in baptism) to be given to a repentance which they have not fulfilled! This is to hold out your hand for merchandise, but not produce the price.'[3] This is what Tertullian is really concerned about, and in my judgment chapter 6 of *De paenitentia* can be understood only when this viewpoint is clearly recognized. Time and again the thing that Tertullian is after comes to the surface: for example in 6.9 we read, 'I do not deny that the divine benefit— i.e. forgiveness of sins—is absolutely assured to such as are on the point of entering the water; but what we have to labour for is that it may be granted to us to attain that blessing. For who will grant to you, a man so renegade to repentance, one single dash of water whatever (let alone the full immersion given in baptism)?'[4] I think it is unnecessary to continue. Tertullian does not set himself against a postponement of baptism, but he does combat the opinion of catechumens who consider that before baptism they do not need to take the Christian ethic so seriously as full Christians: 'Let no one flatter himself on the ground of being assigned to the "recruit classes" of learners, as if on that account he have a licence even now to sin. . . . We are not washed in order that we may escape from sinning, but because we have ceased, since in heart we have been bathed already.'[5] If a temporal delay in relation to baptism is contested by Tertullian, it is not its postponement but its anticipation ('It is fitting that catechumens desire baptism, but not to receive it presumptuously'),[6] namely through the attitude which claims as of right emancipation from sin without any prior aspiration of its own after it. A view exactly comparable to this is found in *De baptismo* 20, namely that anxious striving after cleansing through fasting, night vigil, etc., must precede baptism and continue right up to the time of the confession of sins before baptism, when the deliverance from sin is bestowed.[7]

---

[1] *Omne praeterea cunctationis et tergiversationis erga paenitentiam vitium praesumptio intinctionis inportat.*

[2] *Eruditio non deliquendi*, 6.3 (CC 1, p. 329).

[3] *Quam porro ineptum, quam perversum, paenitentiam non adimplere et veniam delictorum sustinere ; hoc est pretium non exhibere et ad mercem manum emittere*, 6.4 (CC 2, pp. 329 f.).

[4] *Neque ego renuo divinum beneficium, id est abolitionem delictorum, inituris aquam omnimodo salvum esse sed ut eo pervenire contingat elaborandum est. Quis enim tibi tam infidae paenitentiae viro asperginem unam cuiuslibet aquae commodabit?* (CC 2, p. 330).

[5] *Nemo ergo sibi aduletur quia inter auditorum tirocinia deputatur, quasi eo etiamnunc sibi delinquere liceat . . . non ideo abluimur ut delinquere desinamus sed quia desiimus, quoniam iam corde loti sumus*, 6.14, 17 (CC 2, p. 331).

[6] *Itaque audientes optare intinctionem, non praesumere oportet*, 6.20 (CC 2, p. 332).

[7] CC 1, p. 294.

Once more, if the reader can bear the reminder yet again, the consideration of the teaching of Tertullian brings us to the end of the second century AD. The picture we have gained corresponds to that presented in the *Church Order* of Hippolytus and the statements of Origen. In Tertullian's tract *De baptismo*, I would venture to suggest, we catch a glimpse of the very beginnings of infant baptism in Carthage and Africa. About AD 200 there was a movement in that area that desired the baptism even of infants, a movement that was manifestly not very old, for Tertullian's polemic is directed against something *new*; and yet it was so powerful that Tertullian had to enter into open discussion with it. His resistance was unsuccessful; the new powers were too strong and infant baptism spread ever more widely, until fifty years later we find it as the norm. Bishop Fidus, to whom Cyprian wrote,[1] had no doubt as to the necessity of infant baptism; his query concerned only the time for its administration. On the other hand his proposal to select the eighth day for the baptism of the newly-born could be viewed as an indication that at that time in the African Church there was no absolute unanimity concerning the details of infant baptism; and that would provide a yet further hint that it was not a custom handed down from the earliest Fathers but one that had taken its rise from a not too distant time, namely at the end of the second century AD.

[1] Cf. above, p. 46. Jeremias writes (p. 85): 'Tertullian's objections made no impression, not even upon Cyprian of Carthage, who was in other respects so strongly influenced by him.' But Tertullian's opposition should not be dismissed so lightly. What fruits would have matured from it had Tertullian remained in the fellowship of the Great Church cannot be known. The fact that he broke away from it in 207, and from then on violently attacked it, brought into discredit the views and demands on church practice that he had earlier represented; it cut off the possibilities of their development and even indirectly, and contrary to his desires, furthered within the Great Church the theory and practice that he had opposed—in our case the spread of infant baptism.

5

Indirect Testimonies to Infant Baptism in the Second Century?

THE RESULT to which our investigations have so far led remains constant: direct evidence from the Church Fathers for infant baptism begins in the third century—a phenomenon which, we observe in passing, can hardly be accidental.[1] Prior to this we read only of the baptism of adults; infant baptism appears to be excluded, at least so far as anything can be inferred from the texts that have come down to us. It ought to be admitted that the chain of statements so far adduced in the discussion is relatively compact. But we equally admit that a caution has to be entered with regard to the earliest period of the Church, as of course for all others, only it may apply here in even greater measure: the utterances of theological writers only offer glimpses into the life of the Church; the actual life of the communities may have had a different complexion from the impression conveyed by the literature, or it may have possessed additional elements on which the literature is silent. In order therefore to be confident as to our results we must ask whether indications are to be found outside the works of the Church Fathers which, in opposition to them, either prove an earlier existence of infant baptism, or at least make it probable. Jeremias, in part following in the wake of earlier writers, appeals to a whole series of significant statements, originating chiefly in the region of Asia Minor: 'They are of an indirect nature but they confirm each other. The oldest of them takes us back to apostolic times, probably to the years when the Gospels of Matthew and Luke were written.'[2] Some attention must therefore be given to these testimonies, in case the objection be raised that we have left out of account important material and that we have treated the matter too casually.

At first glance the statements look impressive. They yield direct or indirect indications of people having belonged to the Christian Church

---

[1] On this see further below, pp. 101 ff.   [2] p. 59.

for such a long period of time, the impression is involuntarily received that they must have belonged to the Church from the earliest days of their life. When e.g. Polycarp says that he has served Christ eighty-six years;[1] when Polycrates characterizes himself as having lived sixty-five years in the Lord (ἐν κυρίῳ ἔχων);[2] when Justin claims to be able to name 'many men and women' sixty and seventy years old, who 'from childhood have been disciples of the Lord' (ἐκ παίδων ἐμαθητεύθησαν τῷ Χριστῷ) and all their life have remained true to him;[3] when in the Acts of the Martyrs Papylus states that he has been serving the Lord 'from youth up' (ἀπὸ νεότητος),[4] are we not to conclude that all these had received baptism as infants?

First, there should be added to these statements another of which, so far as I am aware, no use has been made in the search after proofs for the existence of infant baptism in the early Church, namely a passage in the *First Letter of Clement*. It surpasses in age all the material adduced by Jeremias and takes us right into the first century. The *Letter of Clement* is a communication from the church of Rome to the church of Corinth in AD 96; it is delivered by the hand of a group of messengers, of whom it is expressly said they 'have walked among us from youth to old age un-blameably'.[5] Anyone who in the year 96 had attained to 'old age'[6] or even only to an advanced age, and who therefore, let us say cautiously, was then 60–70 years old, was born between AD 26 and 36—therefore quite certainly a pagan! The church of Rome was founded between AD 40 and 50.[7] Accordingly the messengers who had lived in Rome as Christians ἀπὸ νεότητος could have been baptized at the earliest when children of four years old, presuming, of course, that they belonged to the church of Rome from the beginning! For ἐν ἡμῖν is certainly to be interpreted as relating to the Christian church at Rome. We therefore come to the conclusion: ἀπὸ νεότητος is to be related quite generally to 'youth', not exclusively to the earliest period of youth, and quite certainly not to the time of infancy. Actually it ought to be quite unnecessary to demonstrate a point like this, but in the light of the consequences which Jeremias draws from the statement of Papylus ἀπὸ νεότητος θεῷ δουλεύω, it is evidently not superfluous. Only by a complicated and laboured exegesis can the needful conclusions

---

[1] *Mart. Pol.* 9.3; Euseb, *HE* IV, 15.20.   [2] Euseb, *HE* V, 24.7.   [3] *Apol.* I, 15.6.

[4] 34 (R. Knopf and G. Krüger, *Ausgewählte Märtyrerakten*³ (Tübingen, 1929) p. 12, lines 26 f.).

[5] Ἀπὸ νεότητος ἀναστραφέντες ἕως γήρους ἀμέμπτως ἐν ἡμῖν, *I Clem.* 63.3; in 65.1 their names are given.

[6] So Arndt and Gingrich under γῆρας.

[7] A date earlier than AD 40 is hardly to be received if the crucifixion of Jesus is to be set in or about the year 30.

be extracted; either it must be maintained that ἕως γήρους is not to be understood literally, or ἐν ἡμῖν must be related generally to Rome and not to the Christian Church there, or ἀμέμπτως has a general moralistic intention and does not denote the Christian 'walk' of the messengers. But a prejudgment of this kind should not be made.

Let us tarry a while among the Acts of the Martyrs. About the remark of Papylus there is no need to say anything more. Jeremias however adduces 'similar sayings' of other martyrs. Euelpistos declared, 'I also received my Christianity from my parents';[1] Hierax similarly, 'I was a Christian long ago and always shall be';[2] and Paion, 'We received from our parents this good confession.'[3] What does this mean in practice? Euelpistos and Paion took over Christianity from their parents; they came from Christian families. As to their baptism, and particularly their baptism as infants, not a word is expressed. Ἔκπαλαι, says Hierax, he has been a Christian. Ἔκπαλαι[4] means, 'long ago, for a long time'—again the same result! Just one more statement should be noted, that of Maximus. It is the only one which gives a more precise indication of time, but it expressly points away from the age of infancy to a later time! Maximus says, *ego non sacrificio nisi soli deo, cui me ab ineunte aetate sacrificasse congratulor*, i.e. 'I do not offer sacrifice except to the one God, to whom, I am glad to say, I have offered sacrifice from early youth.' *Ineunte aetate* at best = 'from early youth on', never 'from birth on'!

The case is similar with the other testimonies brought forward by Jeremias.[5] Most probably Polycrates comes from a Christian family, since in his letter written to Rome *c*. AD 190, in connection with the controversy as to the date of Easter, he is able to allude to the large number of bishops that came from his family. Jeremias, however, does not content himself with this deduction, which of course, contributes nothing to our quest after the age of the administration of baptism. He explains: 'When he continues, "I now, my brethren, have lived in the Lord (ἔχων ἐν κυρίῳ) sixty-five years", we may conclude that he was baptized as a child about AD 125.'[6] Rather I would think that with these words Polycrates intends to indicate nothing more than his age (what a Christian possesses, he has

---

[1] Παρὰ τῶν γονέων δὲ καγὼ παρείληφα Χριστιανὸς εἶναι, 4.7 (Knopf-Krüger, p. 16. 32).

[2] Ἔκπαλαι ἤμην Χριστιανὸς καὶ ἔσομαι, 4.5 (Knopf-Krüger, p. 16. 28). The translation by David Cairns, 'I always have been a Christian . . .' (Jeremias, p. 64 n. 2) is too strong.

[3] Ἀπὸ τῶν γονέων παρειλήφαμεν τὴν καλὴν ταύτην ὁμολογίαν, 4.6 (Knopf-Krüger, p. 16. 30 f.).

[4] See Arndt and Gingrich, p. 242.

[5] It is unnecessary to give detailed consideration to the 'young' (*teneri*) of the Letter of Pliny (see Jeremias, pp. 63 f.): it yields no information and at most relates to children of several years old.

[6] p. 63.

'ἐν κυρίῳ'), to which he calls attention along with the other characteristics which distinguish him (cf. the continuation, 'and I have met with the brethren throughout the world and have gone through every holy Scripture'). If anyone should consider this interpretation too profane, he at least ought to take note that Jeremias' interpretation, 'We may conclude that he was baptized as a child about AD 125,' is at all events read into the text and not out of it. For to belong to the Christian Church for sixty-five years gives no information as to the time of baptism, and does not need to include infant baptism. The same must also be said of the claims made regarding Polycarp, despite the imposing number of eighty-six, and the men and women mentioned by Justin who were sixty and seventy years old. Here again the text is made to yield too much. Justin writes of these Christians, 'They have been disciples of Christ from childhood.'[1] Jeremias interprets, 'The passive of the word μαθητεύειν signifies "becoming a Christian", *Dial* 39.2, with clear reference to baptism.'[2] That is hardly to be admitted. Jeremias cites *Dial*. 39.2,[3] '. . . made disciples to the name of his Christ . . . illuminated through the name of this Christ'; but the second part only of the sequence of thought relates to baptism, the first does not. That in itself excludes the interpretation that Jeremias brings to the passage, quite apart from the fact that ἐκ παίδων ἐμαθητεύθησαν taken as it stands cannot possibly mean, 'they had been baptized as infants', but rather, 'they had been instructed in Christian faith from childhood, and grown up as members of a Christian family.' Jeremias may perhaps reply in objection that he did not say that the men and women of whom Justin speaks had been baptized as *infants*, but rather, 'The men and women mentioned by Justin were baptized "as children" (ἐκ παίδων) in the time between AD 80 and 95;'[4] and shortly before that he had explicitly stated, 'The passive of the word μαθητεύειν signifies "becoming a Christian".' If so, we would then have one of the cases in which Jeremias uses his words in so unprecise a fashion that with the more precise reader they produce favourable associations beyond what the test can bear and beyond that which Jeremias actually intends the reader to receive as proof. But again, if we enquire precisely as to the meaning of the phrase 'as children', we have seen that the answer 'as infants' is excluded; Jeremias has then produced an argument whose effect is contrary to his intention! in the paragraph immediately following he mentions, in connection with the D text of Acts 2.39,[5] the children of Christian parents, who according to Jeremias were confessedly baptized immediately after birth. If Jeremias wants us to

---

[1] οἱ ἐκ παίδων ἐμαθητεύθησαν τῷ Χριστῷ, *Apol.* I, 15.6.
[2] p. 83.   [3] p. 72 n. 2.   [4] p. 72.   [5] See below on this, pp. 85 f.

view the men and women of whom Justin speaks as the children of Christian marriages, then, assuming that the reply we have adduced as possible is conceived as actual, he has given us an example of what he calls 'postponement of baptism', i.e. of the baptism of Christian children at a *later* age. There remains only the possibility of characterizing the men and women as having become Christians through 'missionary baptism'—but in any case we have here an indubitable example of the baptism of children of maturer years. But in that case should Jeremias have brought the men and women of Justin into the discussion at all?

6

The Evidence of the Christian Inscriptions

JEREMIAS refers to early Christian inscriptions on many occasions and devotes considerable space to them in support of his case.[1] Yet at the outset it should be observed that they yield no information, and indeed can give none, concerning the time at which infant baptism took root in the Church. They do not commence until the third century, and by that time infant baptism is in any case attested in Africa, Italy and (possibly) Palestine. When Jeremias therefore bids us consider inscriptions[2] from the third century that emanate from Italy[3] and North Africa,[4] they can impart nothing new to us, at least in so far as the evidence they provide touches on infant baptism. Whether in point of fact they do yield any such evidence is a matter of strongest dissension. Only in a single case do these inscriptions actually speak of an infant. In this example a report is given concerning a child who remained alive for but a few hours.

> Arisus i [n] pace
> natus ora sexta
> bixit s(upra) s(criptas) VIIII.[5]

Jeremias comments on this inscription: 'From the words *in pace* ("in peace") we may infer that the little child who died nine hours after its birth was baptized.'[6] The sceptical could object to him that it is a point requiring proof that *in pace* = 'after the reception of baptism', above all in view of the concept of the holiness of children, which certainly continued to be an accepted belief of that time.[7] If however, this child had been

---

[1] See pp. 41 f., 55 f., 75–80, 85 f., 89–93.
[2] Contrary to the view of F. J. Dölger, whom Jeremias follows, it seems to me that the Eutychian inscription cannot be dated so early as '*c.* AD 200 or shortly after' but belongs to a later time.   [3] See pp. 41 f., 55 f., 76–80.   [4] p. 85.
[5] Diehl, *Inscr. lat. Christ. vet.* II, 4429 A, an inscription coming from Hadrumetum (North Africa), Jeremias, p. 85.   [6] Jeremias, p. 85.   [7] See below, pp. 104 f.

baptized, we would then quite certainly be dealing with an emergency baptism, and Tertullian himself, despite his opposition to infant baptism, regarded that as permissible;[1] accordingly no conclusion as to a general application of infant baptism can be drawn from this example.

Of the other inscriptions adduced by Jeremias three or four can be considered as pertinent to our theme, for the ages of the children to whom these burial inscriptions relate range from eight months to little more than one year.[2] In all other cases the reported ages automatically preclude the inscriptions from our consideration (the ages of these children are two years one month,[3] twelve years (!),[4] two years one month,[5] three years,[6] two years two months[7]). Moreover in these particular inscriptions the fact of baptism is not mentioned, only the Christian profession of the deceased child or of the parents comes to view; consequently no argument for the baptism of these children in infancy can be drawn from them—on the contrary they provide an argument *against it*! Several inscriptions that contain explicit mention of baptism make it clear that these child baptisms were emergency baptisms, and hence that these children at any rate would not have been baptized at this age had they not incurred serious illness. Apronianus, for instance, is baptized shortly before his death at the age of one year nine months five days,[8] Tyche on the very day of her death at the age of one year ten months fifteen days,[9] Irene one week before her death at the age of eleven months six days,[10] while Marcianus, over the age of twelve (!), was baptized one day before his death.[11]

In all these cases baptism is actually mentioned. If these inscriptions had been dated in the fourth century, Jeremias would have regarded them as

---

[1] *De bapt.* 18.4 (CC 1, p. 293).

[2] Diehl II, 3943 (Africa), Jeremias, p. 85; Diehl I, 1611 C (Rome), Jeremias, p. 76; Diehl I, 2264 (Rome), Jeremias, p. 77; also possibly Diehl II, 4464 (Rome?), Jeremias, p. 77. Diehl I, 1520 is too mutilated to permit any inference from it, hence Jeremias goes much too far in his interpretation, p. 77; that *dulcissime nate* must denote 'a child who died at a very early age', in any case is disputable, for it can as well signify a 'very dear son', without any limitation to a very young age. The νήπιος Διονύσιος of *CIG* IV, no. 9574 I would not assign to this age group without hesitation: perhaps rather it should be reckoned in the next one. Similarly the ἀγνὸν παιδίον Kyriakos, *CIG* IV, no. 9801 (Rome), Jeremias, pp. 76 f., is too uncertainly described to determine his age. These children could have been two years old and more and still possess these attributes. Finally the inscription *CIG* IV, no. 9715, which speaks of three twelve-year-old children, does not seem to me to permit a definition such as Dölger gives, 'believers *from birth*' (ΙΧΘΥΣ I, 201); that is represented not by γενετῇ but quite regularly by ἐκ γενετῆς (Jeremias, p. 56, more cautiously says 'It (is) probable that in the case of the three boys also baptism was administered at the earliest age'). πιστοὺς γενέτῃ προέπεμψα probably means, 'I (the father or relative) have sent on (the three twelve-year-old) believers to the father (or relative).'

[3] Jeremias, p. 56.   [4] *Ibid.*   [5] p. 77.   [6] *Ibid.*   [7] p. 78.

[8] Diehl I, 1343, Rome, Jeremias, p. 42.   [9] Diehl I, 1531, Rome, Jeremias, p. 78.

[10] Diehl I, 1532, Jeremias, p. 79. If the baptism should have taken place on Easter Day, the year 261 falls to be considered or 250 (not 251), apart from these 239, and even 323, 334, 345, etc.   [11] Diehl II, 3315, Rome, Jeremias, p. 80.

examples of the conscious postponement of baptism that does in fact meet us in that century.[1] How then does Jeremias fit them into the third century? Since he believes that infant baptism was obligatory for children of Christian parents in the third century, as in the second, he offers the explanation: 'We must conclude that these emergency baptisms were administered to children of non-Christians,' and again: 'In all probability the parents in these cases were pagan.'[2]

On the contrary, this view has all probability against it.[3] In at least one of the three cases Jeremias' presupposition in my judgment does not commend itself as satisfactory. In the Apronianus inscription[4] Jeremias regards the '*D(is) M(anibus) S(acrum)*', lit. 'sacred to (the memory of) the blessed spirit,' as a proof that Florentius, the father named in the inscription, was a pagan,[5] and that the grandmother was responsible for the baptism of the child.[6] This is admittedly possible. But the like cannot be asserted of the Tyche inscription:

> *Tyche dulcis*
> *uixit anno uno*
> *mensibus X, dieb(us) XV.*
> *accepit VIII k[. . .*
> *reddidit die s(upra) s(cripto),*[7]

Nor can it of the Irene inscription:

> *Ir[en]e quae uix(it)*
> *cum p[are]ntibus*
> *suis m(ensibus) X,*[8] *d(iebus) VI.*

[1] On p. 90, Jeremias gives such an interpretation of inscriptions cited from the fourth century concerning children varying in age from eight months to nine years, including even emergency baptisms! [2] p. 80.

[3] Even churches of our day refuse to baptize children of parents who do not belong to the Church. The inscriptions must have at least concerned children of mixed marriages, i.e. of parents of whom one was Christian and the other pagan, or of a family that otherwise stood in a positive relation to a particular church because some of its members were Christian.

[4] Rendered into English on p. 42 thus:
> Dedicated to the departed.
> Florentius made this inscription
> for his worthy son Apronianus who lived
> one year and nine months and five days.
> As he was truly loved by his grandmother
> and she knew that his death was imminent,
> she asked the church that he might
> depart from the world as a believer.

[5] In the inscriptions given on pp. 85 and 77, however, the *DMS* or *DM* occurs without any such estimate of its significance; the inscription on p. 77 in any case comes from a catacomb. [6] p. 42.   [7] Diehl I, 1531, Rome, Jeremias, p. 78.

[8] So according to Diehl and Dölger; Jeremias reads XI, which is (at least according to the reproduction) quite possible.

acc(epit) VII id. April.
et redd(idit) id. A[p]ril.[1]

for in both these cases the text betrays no indication of a purely pagan marriage; the terminology is such as Christians commonly used. Jeremias, pursuing the idea of the non-Christian origin of the Irene inscription, suggests the following solution: 'It might perhaps have happened that the illness of the little child, who, as is so touchingly said, "lived with her parents eleven months six days", gave them the impulse to ask for baptism, which the little Irene survived by only six days.'[2] This is a highly ingenious interpretation and much could be said about it; while it should not be dismissed out of hand, it is undeniable that having regard to the text, it is pure hypothesis.[3]

We turn to the third of the inscriptions that fall within our purview, reminding ourselves once more that the three inscriptions which are here being reviewed are the only ones that expressly mention baptism. It runs:

Pasto[r et T]i[t]iana et (dove) *Marciana et* (leaf)
Chr[e]st[e Mar]ciano filio benemerenti [in]
XP.dn., fec[eru]n[t]qui uixit annus XII m(enses) II et d[ies . . .]
qui cra[tiam] accepit d.n. die XII ka[l.O]ctob[r]es [Ma]
[rini]ano (et) Paterno II coss. et rede[dit] XI ka[l.ss.?]
uibas inter sanctis in a [eternum].

Now this inscription, by the nature of its text as by its mention of the dove and (ivy?) leaf or fish,[4] shows itself unambiguously to be Christian (cf. lines 2 f., 'a well deserving son in Christ the Lord'; 4, 'received grace'; 6, 'alive among the saints in eternity'); the possibility of pagan parents commissioning such an inscription is absolutely to be rejected (it will surely not be objected that the Christian terminology is to be credited to the mason who chose it of his own accord?). No, the theory that these inscriptions relate to the baptisms of children of pagan and not Christian parents cannot be maintained. This particular child of Christian parents in Rome was not baptized till he was over twelve years old! The inscription actually shatters the thesis that infant baptism was administered to

---

[1] Diehl I, 1532, Jeremias, p. 79.
[2] p. 79. He does not comment on the parallel case of Tyche; presumably he would say the same of it, although the duplication would not make his solution the more probable.
[3] From the point of view of the way baptism was administered at that time it has probability against it. The situation presupposed by Jeremias is derived from modern usages and ideas.
[4] So Marucchi, *Epigrafia Cristiana*, 1910, p. 99, no. 55.

Christian children, and at the same time it tears a very large hole in the idea that infant baptism was obligatory in the third century; it further demonstrates that, despite the evidence provided by the *Church Order* of Hippolytus[1] and Cyprian, the custom of baptizing very little children was not observed without exception in Italy at that time (correspondingly the same might have applied in Africa and other provinces). It is perhaps superfluous to mention that this inscription is dated by the mention of the consuls in the year 268 and that therefore it cannot be pushed off to the fourth century. Moreover it shows conclusively how impossible the theory of Jeremias is, that all baptisms at a later age were of such as were converted from without, and that children of Christian parents were normally baptized as children or infants.

We have now completed the review of material from the early centuries offered in support of infant baptism—at least, I hope that nothing has been overlooked. The result is plain, if I may be permitted to repeat it once more: the first unambiguous testimonies for infant baptism emerge about the middle of the first half of the third century. This unambiguity, however, applies only to the writings or writers concerned. For despite the thesis maintained by Jeremias, the inscriptions, which are the sole testimonies we possess besides the patristic writings, do not permit us to assume that the usage attested in the *Church Order* of Hippolytus and by Cyprian was compulsory for all Italy and all Africa; indeed they do not even allow us to presume that the situation presupposed in the *Church Order* of Hippolytus was valid for all Rome, since the Marcianus inscription comes from Rome. The inscriptions, far from supporting the position of Jeremias, decisively weaken it. If, on the other hand, appeal should be made to these inscriptions (and their number could easily be multiplied) for the view that infant baptism was known, or its existence is demanded by these three sources, but that it was only *partially* observed, and that along with this practice baptisms at a later age were quite usual and remained widespread, this position would not be shattered by the inscriptions; indeed, it could appeal for support to the fact that the *Church Order* of Hippolytus is itself acquainted with the baptism of children of maturer years as well as with the practice of infant baptism.

[1] Presupposing that that section really does go back to Hippolytus, see above, pp. 49 f.

7

Paul and the Primitive Church

THE NEW TESTAMENT evidence has to this point been left out of the discussion. The earliest testimony with which we have dealt is that of the *Didache*, written *c.* AD 100 or early in the second century, and the *First Letter of Clement*, *c.* AD 96. Does the New Testament perhaps provide a counter-argument against the result to which we have been so far led? It would hardly seem so; rather the view we have expounded receives decisive support from its precipitate in the oldest New Testament evidence that has come down to us, namely I Cor. 7.14. We have already noted[1] that Jeremias, in the German edition of his book, reached the conclusion, 'From I Cor. 7.14c, it appears that Paul knows nothing of a baptism of children born to Christian parents.'[2] In the English edition he withdraws this view and states, 'We must be content with the conclusion that I Cor. 7.14c bears no reference to baptism.'[3] Jeremias does not stand alone in this interpretation; Kümmel, for example, had earlier declared, 'I Cor. 7.14 allows no kind of conclusion concerning the practice of infant baptism, not even in a restricted measure.'[4] Now it is true that Paul does not make any explicit statement in I Cor. 7.14 as to whether children are baptized or not; nevertheless I cannot assent to Kümmel's position without qualification, for it seems to me that more can be gleaned from I Cor. 7.14 than he admits. In this passage Paul refers to the holiness (not 'cleanness', as one might have expected from the foregoing ἀκάθαρτος) of children in a pagan-Christian marriage with such definiteness, even making it a proof of his thesis of the holiness of the non-Christian partner through the Christian, that some quite firm conclusions follow from it. If Paul's statement applies to children of a mixed marriage, it must apply at least as much to children of a purely Christian marriage. The mixed marriages that Paul has in view are not regarded as dominated by the Christian element; on

---

[1] See above, p. 34.   [2] p. 54, German ed.   [3] p. 48.
[4] In Lietzmann's commentary *An Die Korinther* (Handbuch zum Neuen Testament, vol. 9), 4th ed. by W. G. Kümmel, 1949, p. 177.

the contrary the Apostle recognizes that the pagan member may possibly desire a divorce. The Christian spouse is not to resist that, for it is by no means sure that he (or she) will succeed in winning the non-Christian partner (7.15 f.). Further, in the light of these circumstances it is altogether possible that some at least of the children of these mixed marriages are not baptized (assuming for the moment that the custom of infant baptism is in existence at the time) or that they are maintained by the non-Christian parent in his own (heathen) form of faith. Where that is so it follows that Paul's unqualified statement about the holiness of all the children of the mixed marriage rules out the requirement of baptism as the presupposition of this holiness, even supposing that the rite was applied to children. This conclusion, although an inference from the text and not actually stated in it, seems to me without objection, if not actually compelling.

Whatever one's view of this interpretation, so much is clear: a baptism of children in the Pauline churches cannot be derived from I Cor. 7.14, still less a baptism of infants. We shall have to defer for the present[1] consideration of the 'materialistic conception of holiness', to quote Kümmel as the most radical exponent of a restrictive view of I Cor. 7.14,[2] which characterizes Paul's view of children (Kümmel believes that there is no necessity to trace it back to proselyte baptism but holds it to be a reflection of popular ideas).[3]

It is really surprising that Jeremias in the English edition of his work still stands by the claim that I Cor. 7.14c belongs to the realm of Jewish ritual language. Earlier it was of significance as supporting Jeremias' deductions, but now that is no longer the case. I do not feel competent to judge the details of the Jewish parallels cited by Jeremias,[4] but I have some considerable and fundamental misgivings as to his declarations on I Cor. 7.14c. When he writes of this verse, 'That is Jewish and not Pauline usage,'[5] at most the assertion may be true of the terminological usage, but it does not apply to the practical attitude adopted by Paul. It should be noted that the passage is not concerned with purely Christian marriages but with marriages between a Christian and an unbelieving partner. The Christian partner sanctifies the pagan; that is proved by the unquestioned fact that the children of this 'mixed marriage' are holy, not unclean. One need only transpose the presuppositions behind I Cor. 7.12 ff. from the Christian sphere to the Jewish to see that the deduction of Jeremias does not hold good at the vital point: the idea of a legitimate marriage between a Jewish and a non-Jewish spouse is impossible to late Judaism—and

---

[1] See below, pp. 104 f. [2] *Op. cit.*, p. 176. [3] *Op. cit.*, p. 177.
[4] p. 47, cf. also pp. 37 ff. [5] p. 46.

F

indeed to Judaism generally—to say nothing about the notion that a non-Jewish partner may continue in his own faith and yet be looked on as holy, and that children from this marriage are holy, whether they follow the faith of the Jewish parent or not. From the aspect of method also it would appear that strong reservations require to be made respecting the position taken by Jeremias. Of course it is possible that the Jewish or Jewish-Christian pattern of the Jerusalem church exercised an influence on the Pauline churches, but the denial of the validity of the ceremonial law makes it more than likely that the observance of the regulations pertaining to proselytes also fell into desuetude. When Jeremias deduces from Acts 21.21 that the primitive church in Jerusalem circumcised male children born in their midst, that seems to me eminently suitable,[1] but such an admission says nothing at all about Paul and his churches. As Haenchen rightly observes on this passage, 'According to Luke's representation, the elders plainly did not believe the charge.'[2] The engagement to defray the costs for the Nazarite vow of four Jewish Christians, which Paul was asked to bear and to which he consented, serves to contradict the widespread allegation that Paul was leading the Diaspora Jews away from the law. Yet Haenchen's assertion at this point: 'That Paul advised against the circumcision of Jewish children is improbable,'[3] is not altogether convincing in the light of Gal. 2 and the Letter to the Galatians as a whole. Gal. 2.13, with its sharp criticism of the λοιποὶ Ἰουδαῖοι, leaves one with the impression that Paul regarded the table fellowship of Jewish and Gentile Christians, and thus the setting aside of the ceremonial law,[4] as normative for his churches.[5] In these Pauline churches, which from time to time included a certain proportion of Jews, a literal observance by the Jewish Christians of the law's demands, especially of those relating to foods, would have made a division unavoidable, or at least it would have caused

[1] Moreover it follows that for girls born in the earliest Church nothing whatever was prescribed, since no rite parallel to circumcision was laid down for them in the law—they grew up in the Church automatically, a circumstance that must not be overlooked. Here we have from the beginning even in Jewish Christian churches a situation which helped to prepare for that which we have assumed to exist in the early Church generally, and which formed a transition to it. If the male offspring are stressed in Judaism, the same does not hold good of early Christianity, in which women without doubt played a considerable role; evidently suspicion fell on it through Montanism (and Gnosticism) and a depreciation of the place of women penetrated the Church from Judaism; of this latter there are some early hints in I Corinthians and the Pastoral Epistles.

[2] Die Apostelgeschichte (Meyer's Kritisch-Exegetischer Kommentar über das NT), 12th ed., Göttingen, 1959, p. 542.

[3] p. 540.

[4] Before the arrival of the emissaries of James, and also of Peter and Barnabas, the λοιποὶ Ἰουδαῖοι enjoyed table fellowship with the non-Jews; the same condition could well have existed in the other Pauline churches as in Antioch.

[5] For which reason the abandonment of circumcision necessarily followed.

an unendurable complication in the life of a community.[1] If the circumcision of Timothy is recorded in Acts 16.3, the form of statement in the narrative seems to me to reflect that we have to do with an exception in this case, not the rule. The Letter to the Galatians protests against Gentile Christians who take on themselves, if only in part, the observation of the law (presumably under the influence of emissaries from the Mother Church similar to those who, according to Gal. 2, came to Antioch). Not only the sharpness of the polemic but also the absolute language of the Letter appears to rule out any idea of the validity of the law, even for Christians in the Pauline churches who come out of Judaism, just as (to come back to the original subject) it excludes a continuous application of the prescriptions formerly observed concerning proselytes.

Here is the place perhaps for a word on the question as to whether the application of circumcision to male infants among Jews and in the primitive church in Jerusalem could have formed a valid precedent for the practice of infant baptism. Despite all the parallels which Jeremias draws between 'the Jewish conversion theology connected with proselyte baptism'[2] and the early Christian baptismal theology,[3] the probability is really very small. Certainly it is likely that the primitive community in Jerusalem applied circumcision to children born among them in a manner parallel to its continued observance of the prescriptions of the ceremonial law. But however tempting it may be to draw a straight line from the circumcision of infants to the baptism of infants, i.e. to consider infant baptism as the direct continuation of circumcision, it is not possible to do this on the basis of the historical evidence. First, we have no information at all nor proof of any kind that in the Jerusalem church circumcision *and* baptism were administered at the same time. Secondly the influence of the Palestinian Jewish-Christian church on the other churches decreased to an extraordinary extent, even in the first century. In the Pauline churches, as in those of the 'third type' (the Gentile-Christian churches which were not of Paul's founding), even where they had their beginnings in Diaspora Judaism, the ceremonial law and the circumcision bound up with it did not remain in force; hence there is no reason to postulate among them any further effect of circumcision, i.e. its continuation in a substitute form as the baptism of infants.

Nevertheless Jeremias now affirms twice over, with a truly astonishing

[1] Naturally it is right that a continuation of the practice of circumcision by Jewish Christian members of the Pauline churches would not disturb the life of the church, as also an observance of the food laws by them at the Agape. Nevertheless it does not seem to me to fit I Cor. 7.14. Circumcision could not be hidden from the church, even if it was performed in the family circle.   [2] p. 36.   [3] pp. 36 ff.

assurance in view of the nature of the evidence, that Col. 2.11 proves that
baptism took the place of circumcision, consequently it is to be presumed
that infants were baptized in both the Pauline churches and in the primitive church at Jerusalem. He writes, 'Since, as Col. 2.11 f. tells us, in the
Christian Church baptism was the rite which replaced circumcision, we
must conclude that the fact that the children mentioned in I Cor. 7.14c
were "holy" from their birth does not preclude the possibility that they
were baptized.'[1] And again, 'Since Paul designates baptism as the ritual
which replaces circumcision (Col. 2.11 . . .) it is very probable that these
children were baptized.'[2] In face of these statements it is difficult to repress
the question whether Col. 2.11 really does contain what Jeremias reads out
of it. I confess I cannot find it there. That the (adult) members of the
pauline churches were baptized before their entry into the Church is
obvious. Where pagans were involved it may be feasible to follow Jeremias
and say that baptism is the 'ritual which replaced circumcision'. But what
about the Jew, who has already been circumcised and then becomes baptized? This example alone, to say nothing of the women, is enough to
show that in Col. 2.11 Paul did not have in mind the setting aside of circumcision by baptism. He uses comparisons in his delineation of Christian baptism and tries to describe to the (adult!) recipients of the Letter
the rite and its effect by means of pictorial statements; children are clearly
not in view of this passage, still less infants; they fall completely outside
the writer's field of vision.

A few remarks on Acts 2.38 f. ought perhaps to be added, as a kind of
appendix. Jeremias considers that the passage has come from the 'Jewish-
Christian sphere'.[3] From it he concludes that we have here 'a witness for
the practice of infant baptism in apostolic times, at any rate in the time of
the composition of Luke's twofold work; that is to say for the baptism of
children of Jewish parents on their admission into the Christian Church.'[4]
The question whether in fact we ought to ascribe this passage to the
'Jewish-Christian sphere' will be variously answered, according to our
estimate of the speeches of Peter at Pentecost, reproduced in the Acts of
the Apostles, as historical or as a product of the author of the work; this,
however, is hardly our concern.[5] Jeremias maintains: 'At the most one
can ask if in Acts 2.38 f. an age-limit is indirectly presupposed. H.
Windisch reckoned that here older children must be thought of, namely
such as are ripe for the repentance mentioned in 2.38 and can prophesy

---

[1] p. 47.   [2] p. 48.   [3] German ed. p. 57; ET 'Jewish Christian Church', p. 40.   [4] p. 40.
[5] That the question is answered by not a few exegetes in a manner other than by
Jeremias is well known.

(2.17).[1] This limitation is however highly improbable because the salvation from the final judgment mediated by baptism (2.40; cf. 2.21) excludes any limitation of age.'[2] Admittedly the interpretation of the τέκνα mentioned by Peter in the sense of 'descendants' is 'conceivable for the time of Luke. But the context speaks against it.'[3] For the ἐπαγγελία of which Peter speaks is the promise of Joel 2.28 which Peter cites in Acts 2.17. 'Thus the children are not coming generations, but the sons and daughters of the hearers. Since the gift of the Spirit (2.38) is linked to baptism, 2.39 contains the challenge to have the children baptized also.'[4] I must admit that I cannot share the assurance with which one conclusion here is drawn from another.

Jeremias actually goes a step further than this. In 2.39 Codex Bezae changes the person and writes, ἡμῖν γάρ ἐστιν ἡ ἐπαγγελία καὶ τοῖς τέκνοις ἡμῶν, whereas the text unequivocally reads ὑμῖν and ὑμῶν. We must of course be careful, says Jeremias, 'not to base too far-reaching conjectures on a variant reading, but on the other hand we must not simply ignore it, as is usually done. The most natural explanation of the variant is that the formulation "Be baptized every one of you . . . for the promise is to us and our children" came naturally to the redactor's pen, because the baptism of Christian children was a custom taken for granted.'[5] Let us begin with a consideration of the last deduction, which provides Jeremias with a witness to infant baptism 'before AD 150' in the West. I do not believe we can draw such conclusions. If we but examine how Codex D treats ὑμῖν in other places in Peter's speech, we shall almost certainly feel that Jeremias is trying to extort too much out of the textual variant in Acts 2.39. In 2.17 ὑμῶν appears four times; D replaces it twice by αὐτῶν (υἱοί and θυγατέρες αὐτῶν), twice it leaves it out altogether (after νεανίσκοι and πρεσβύτεροι). The same thing happens in 2.38: D reads here εἰς ἄφεσιν ἁμαρτιῶν instead of εἰς ἄφεσιν τῶν ἁμαρτιῶν ὑμῶν. Indeed, the first hand of D in 2.22 goes so far as to write: Ἰησοῦν τὸν Ναζωραῖον, ἄνδρα δεδοκιμασμένον ἀπὸ τοῦ θεοῦ εἰς ἡμᾶς δυνάμεσι καὶ τέρασι καὶ σημείοις. When we see how D here and in various other passages endeavours to make the text relevant by directly relating it to the reader or hearer, even in contexts where it is quite impossible (as 2.22), we shall not be inclined to regard the change of text in 2.39 as reflecting a practice of infant- or child-baptism in that time. Indeed, we may even be led to doubt the whole interpretation of Jeremias and consider that not only the textual variant but the text itself has consequences that he has not envisaged.

[1] H. Windisch, 'Zum Problem der Kindertaufe im Urchristentum', ZNW 28, 1929, p. 123. [2] p. 41. [3] p. 40. [4] Ibid. [5] p. 72.

Briefly it should be pointed out that not a word about the baptism of children occurs here (2.38), but only of the baptism of the (adult!) hearers, who are exhorted to repent and get baptized. After that the gift of the Holy Spirit is made known to them, whose operations they had witnessed in the Pentecostal speaking with tongues. Then follows the statement (2.39) that the promise is for them—'and,' the context continues, 'for your children'. Manifestly the τέκνοις corresponds to the υἱοὶ ὑμῶν and the θυγατέρες ὑμῶν of Acts 2.17 (= Joel 2.28) and therefore has been determined by the Old Testament prophecy.[1] But more, the text states that the promise applies not alone to the τέκνοις but 'to all who are far (πᾶσιν τοῖς εἰς μακράν), everyone whom the Lord our God may call'. Contrary to Jeremias, the children here surely denote descendants, as the clause that follows emphasizes, i.e. it is to be understood in a temporal and not local sense; πᾶσιν τοῖς εἰς μακράν refers to coming generations.[2]

---

[1] Jeremias himself states this. 'The "promise" of which v. 39 says that it is valid also for the children, is in fact the promise of Joel which was mentioned in 2.17–21, the promise, namely, that God will pour out his Spirit upon all flesh and that "Your sons and daughters will prophesy" (Acts 2.17 = Joel 2.28)' (p. 40). Nevertheless he does not draw out the consequences of this but makes the τέκνα ὑμῶν a testimony for the practice of infant baptism at that time.

[2] Cf. Arndt and Gingrich, p. 488, and the comparative material there adduced.

8

The 'Oikos-Formula'

THE SO-CALLED 'oikos-formula' plays a great part in present-day apologetic for the belief that children and/or infants were baptized in New Testament times. Jeremias places his exposition of the matter right at the beginning of his book. Is it possible, then, that we should recognize in this formula a relatively reliable support for the practice of infant baptism in the New Testament era?

Our best recourse is to begin with a sober estimate of the relevant New Testament passages. According to Bruder's concordance the term οἶκος appears 112 times with a breadth of signification corresponding to the Hebrew equivalent *bayit*. It is perhaps not superfluous to take a brief glance at the New Testament passages in which οἶκος appears, and to see how they are related. On sixty occasions in the New Testament the word possesses its fundamental meaning of 'house, dwelling, at home', etc. Twelve times it denotes οἶκος Ἰσραήλ, Ἰακώβ, Δαυίδ, Ἰούδα, i.e. it represents the tribe or family. The combination οἶκος τοῦ Θεοῦ = the Temple is found nine times, and it denotes the Christian Church eight times.[1] Once οἶκος = 'possession', i.e. that which is in the house. In a whole series of passages its meaning is not certain or is colourless, e.g. Luke 9.61; 10.5; 12.52; 16.4; 19.9 (cf. 19.5); Acts 2.36; 8.3; 10.22 (cf. 10.30; 11.12 f.); I Tim. 3.4, 5, 12; 5.4; for our purpose these may be omitted from consideration. Similarly Heb. 11.7, which speaks of Noah making an ark εἰς σωτηρίαν τοῦ οἴκου αὐτοῦ, may be excluded; the passage may even give a hint that οἶκος can only be used of adults![2]

Thus out of the total number of 112 passages there remain but nine more in which οἶκος possesses the meaning found in Greek usage since Homer, 'family', i.e. the people who are in the house. In three places οἶκος in this sense appears without any further characteristic: in II Tim. 1.16,

---

[1] The passages in Hebrews may be reckoned in the first category, the οἶκος πνευματικός of I Peter 2.5 is drawn into the second.
[2] Gen. 6 f. speaks only of adults, not of children!

Paul wishes blessing on the οἶκος of Onesiphorus, because Onesiphorus has helped him in his imprisonment; in II Tim. 4.19 greetings are passed on to this οἶκος of Onesiphorus; and in Tit. 1.11 it is said of the opponents, against whom the polemic is directed, that they bring ὅλους οἴκους into ruin.

In I Cor. 1.16 we move for the first time into an area where the 'oikos-formula' could yield something for our investigation of infant baptism. Paul there says that besides Crispus and Gaius he also baptized τὸν Στεφανᾶ οἶκον. The statements made by Paul in this passage are set in the context of the quarrels at Corinth and are to be considered as absolutely correct ('beyond them I cannot think of anyone else I baptized'). Admittedly no declarations are made concerning the οἶκος of Stephanas, but indirectly a noteworthy commentary on the use of οἶκος is provided.[1] For the Crispus, who meets us here as the only person baptized by Paul, appears again in the report of the Acts of the Apostles concerning Paul's stay in Corinth. In 18.8 we read, 'Crispus, who held office in the synagogue, became a believer in the Lord σὺν ὅλῳ τῷ οἴκῳ αὐτοῦ.' That the same person is in view in both places can hardly be doubted. In I Cor. Paul looks back on his total stay in Corinth; that he actually baptized Crispus alone and not his οἶκος also seems to be quite certain, especially as the οἶκος is expressly mentioned[2] in the case of Stephanus. What are we to make of this? Either Acts is mistaken and the οἶκος of Crispus was not baptized, or this baptism was administered by a companion of Paul,[3] or the family and its retainers came into the Church but only the head of the family received the baptism, which was considered sufficient. Whichever of these three possibilities is preferred the result is clear, that when Acts 18.8 is brought into the context there is very little hand-hold for a proof of infant baptism.

Four passages in the Book of Acts remain—out of the 112 with which we began. They are all set in the narratives of the conversion of Cornelius in Caesarea, of Lydia the seller of purple and of the keeper of the prison, the latter two living in Philippi. But in my view these three reports offer

---

[1] Moreover a hint of the facts of this situation is provided which, so far as I am aware, is not so much as mentioned by any of the proponents of the 'oikos-formula'. For in I Cor. 16.15 Stephanas comes before us again, together with his οἰκία. οἰκία here = οἶκος. Paul exhorts the Corinthian church to be submissive to the instructions given by the οἰκία of Stephanas. It is the ἀπαρχὴ τῆς 'Ασίας and attends to the διακονία, i.e. the leadership of the Church. That οἰκία = οἶκος in this passage relates only to adults needs no argument. With the best will in the world children cannot be included in this ministry of leading the church—to say nothing of infants!

[2] And this οἶκος (= οἰκία of I Cor. 16.15) Paul *has* baptized!

[3] Silas or Timothy, cf. 18.5; but is such a distinction in the mission situation thinkable? The head of the house' is baptized by Paul himself but the wife and children, if he had such, are baptized by the helpers. Such a division could be imagined only where the ὅλος οἶκος related to the entire domestic staff.

more problems in connection with the 'oikos-formula' than has apparently been realized. For example, looking at them purely externally, a baptism of an οἶκος is explicitly stated only in the case of Lydia: 'She was baptized καὶ (πᾶς? D, etc.) ὁ οἶκος αὐτῆς (16.15). Of the jailor it is said: ἐβαπτίσθη αὐτὸς καὶ οἱ αὐτοῦ ἅπαντες (πάντες, C,KD, etc.) (16.33). The 'oikos-formula' only indirectly comes into view here; P45 offers as a variant ὁ οἶκος αὐτοῦ ὅλος, and Paul and Silas at the end of the narrative demand: 'Believe on the Lord Jesus, and you will be saved σὺ καὶ ὁ οἶκός σου', 16.31, and the comment is added, 'He exulted πανοικεὶ πεπιστευκὼς τῷ θεῷ', 16.34, for which D gig read, σὺν τῷ οἴκῳ αὐτοῦ, etc. In the report of the baptism of Cornelius and in the whole account of the events that took place in his house the term οἶκος is not used at all; it is introduced indirectly by Peter in his report at Jerusalem (11.14): the angel had declared to Cornelius that he was to summon Peter from Joppa, adding, 'He will tell you words by which you will be saved σὺ καὶ πᾶς ὁ οἶκός σου' (exactly the same singular form as is used of the Philippian jailor, 16.31 and 34). It should further be noted that in the introductory narrative, 10.2, Cornelius is said to have been 'a religious man, and he and his whole family joined in the worship of God' (εὐσεβὴς καὶ φοβούμενος τὸν θεὸν σὺν παντὶ τῷ οἴκῳ αὐτοῦ.

A careful examination of the facts seems to me to lead to the very plausible conclusion that in the single passage where the baptism of an οἶκος is directly mentioned, the οἶκος was that of an unmarried woman or of a widow, and therefore that in this οἶκος there were either no children at all, or at least there were no little children or infants. Acts speaks in such exclusive terms of Lydia in 16.14 f. that the possibility of a husband being in the background is prohibited: *she* is the one whose vocation is described ('Lydia, a dealer in purple fabric from the city of Thyatira', v. 14); *she* requests Paul to take lodgings in *her* house ('If you have judged me to be a believer in the Lord, come and stay in my house', v. 15); no other conclusion therefore seems possible to me. If one felt so inclined, it could be assumed that the husband was away travelling, perhaps for the purchase of raw materials and the like for his business. But that is a counsel of despair; he would then come back and find that his entire family—including his household servants—had renounced their former religion[1] and been converted to Christianity. A surprise of that kind, and so independent an action of a wife while temporarily in charge of the household, may be dismissed from consideration.

[1] Probably they were adherents of the synagogue, cf. 16.14, Lydia was 'a worshipper of God'.

Children or the very young or infants could be brought into this household only by way of appeal to the slaves who belonged to it. Admittedly Jeremias could write, 'In view of the general sociological picture we have received of the oldest communities of the missionary church, it is extremely unlikely that the households of Cornelius, of the keeper of the prison in Philippi, of Lydia, of Crispus the leader of the synagogue and of Stephanas ever included a considerable group of slaves, to whom the words ὅλος, πᾶς, ἅπαντες could refer. Accordingly the natural conclusion is that we should take these additional terms to refer to all the children of the house.'[1] But this does not seem right to me. I would incline to the view that the existence of domestic slaves, as of an extensive household generally, is virtually certain alike for Lydia, who must have conducted her business with some assistants at least, the Philippian jailor, for the centurion Cornelius in Caesarea, and the synagogue leader Crispus. Doubtless the early Christian churches gained their recruits chiefly from the lower classes, but the very names we have been discussing provide for all who are interested in the social strata of primitive Christianity clear examples of representatives of higher classes in the churches. In Paul's description of the composition of the church of Corinth he does not say that there were no 'wise men, judged by human standards, powerful and high born' in the Church, but only that there were 'not many' of that order among them. In the case of those we have named, their calling or position, to judge by what we know of those times, automatically demands that we assume the existence of domestic staffs, i.e. slaves. It would accordingly be quite possible to relate ὅλος, πᾶς, ἅπαντες only to slaves—and the children postulated by Jeremias would be excluded. On the other hand these slaves might have been married and had newly-born children.

Before we start on a road of this sort, however, we should look again at the most detailed of the three pertinent conversion stories, namely that of Cornelius, and ask whether something does not emerge out of the relatively large number of details at our disposal that will show who can be understood as converted and baptized in this context of the 'oikos-formula'. In Acts 11.14 Peter reports the angel's declaration to Cornelius that he 'and his whole house' would be saved through the preaching of the Apostle. Thereupon Cornelius sends for Peter, Acts 10.7 f., and prepares himself for his arrival and the fulfilment of the promise. But in what manner? Acts 10.24 narrates with all clarity what kind of an assembly was awaiting Peter on his entry into the house of Cornelius: 'Cornelius was expecting them and had called together his relatives and close friends.' It was these

[1] p. 20.

'relatives' and 'close friends' whom Peter found gathered with Cornelius (10.27); it was to them he spoke, on them the Holy Spirit fell (10.44), so that they spoke in tongues (10.46), and it was they who became baptized (10.47 f.). We are not dealing here with an assembly of the οἶκος with parents, children and domestic servants, but with a meeting of like-minded adults coming from different families! Of children, or the very young, or infants there is not even a hint here; nor have we to presuppose the presence of slaves in this circle. Women will undoubtedly have been there, including the wife of Cornelius if he had one, but more than this cannot justly be concluded from the text. If Acts 11.14 speaks of the salvation of the οἶκος, this salvation, *so far as* the slaves belonging to the house or children are included, is understood indirectly; the conversion of Cornelius will have the effect of making theirs to follow, or even embraces theirs: the 'house' is saved when the head of the house is saved.[1]

The conversion of the Philippian jailor remains to be considered. In view of the lack of concrete statements in the text I would not attempt a description of the circle of those involved in 16.32 (σὺν πᾶσιν τοῖς ἐν τῇ οἰκίᾳ αὐτοῦ), 16.33 (αὐτὸς καὶ οἱ αὐτοῦ ἅπαντες) and 16.34 (ἠγαλλιάσατο (!) πανοικεὶ πεπιστευκὼς (!) τῷ θεῷ, which relates only to the coming to faith of the keeper of the prison!). That slaves were included in the group seems to me on general grounds to be certain (cf. 16.29!); that the keeper of the prison was married is equally likely, but whether he had children, or whether little children or infants were in the house, obviously cannot be determined. The report in 16.32, that the jailor received baptismal instruction 'with all who were in his house', does not exactly demand the assumption that infants were included in these πᾶσιν. The actual composition of the οἶκος of the Philippian prison keeper remains obscure, despite the length of the report preserved to us.

In any case the data that can be gathered from the New Testament seem to me in no way to justify the confidence with which the existence of infant baptism in New Testament times, or even quite generally of the baptism of children, is derived nowadays from the 'oikos-formula'. I would even contest whether we have any right to talk about an 'oikos-formula' in the New Testament, as Jeremias and Stauffer and many others do at present. I consider that the facts of the case make that plain enough. The elevation of this 'oikos-formula' to a theological status seems to me to be utterly unsatisfactory. Jeremias writes thus: 'When after these observations we turn to the New Testament, we must keep in mind that the New Testa-

---

[1] The corresponding passages dealing with the conversion of the Philippian jailor are built up in an exactly parallel manner.

ment *oikos*-formula is very early. It occurs as early as AD 54 in Paul (I Cor. 1.16), and is to be found independently of Paul in Luke, and is therefore to be regarded as a pre-Pauline formula. Thus it comes from a time in which the majority of the members of the churches came from the synagogue and from the circle of the "God-fearers" loosely attached thereto. If we grasp this, we shall have to agree with Stauffer's conclusion, that the New Testament *oikos*-formula was adopted from the Old Testament cultic language (and in particular, we may say, from the terminology of circumcision) and introduced into the formal language employed in the primitive Christian rite of baptism; it has the same form and meaning as the old biblical ritual formula, i.e. it includes small children as well as others.'[1] This seems to me greatly exaggerated, and not alone with respect to the circle of people involved. In the usage of οἶκος with which we are concerned we have to do with a linguistic phenomenon that runs completely parallel to the profane (since Homer!) and that is not to be distinguished from it. The 'family' and 'inhabitants of the house', etc., have no theological aura about them, and equally the overwhelming majority of the *oikos*-passages of the New Testament say no more about the οἶκος than would be the case if the texts stood in a profane context. In my opinion the sole exceptions to this are seen in those places where we read of the churches κατ᾽ οἶκον, and in passages in which the οἶκος θεοῦ (whether in relation to the Temple or the Church) and the οἶκος ᾽Ισραήλ, Δαυίδ, etc., are spoken of. But these fall outside the area of our interest, and they are not taken into account by the advocates of the '*oikos*-formula', just as the οἰκία-passages, whose relation to the οἶκος-sayings surely ought to be investigated,[2] are entirely left aside.

Now E. Stauffer, in an important article written for the clergy,[3] with great emphasis represented the character of the '*oikos*-formula' as a 'ritual formula' of the Old Testament. This is not the place nor is there the possibility of entering into a discussion of the evidence presented by the Septuagint. For οἶκος appears with such preponderate frequency (Hatch and Redpath used more than twenty-eight columns for it in their concordance of the Septuagint!), and it represents so many Hebrew equivalents (Hatch and Redpath mention twenty-one), a full discussion of the data would have to be very comprehensive. Yet even without such a detailed

---

[1] p. 21.
[2] See, besides the passages considered on p. 88 n. 1 (John 4.53; Phil. 4.22) I Tim. 5.13; II Tim. 3.6; Matt. 12.24; Mark 3.25; Matt. 13.57; Mark 6.4, etc. The result, if we may anticipate it, would not be different from the investigation of the οἶκος passages in the New Testament in the manner we have indicated above.
[3] 'Zur Kindertaufe in der Urkirche', *Deutsches Pfarrerblatt* 49, 1949, pp. 152–4.

investigation one thing can be asserted: of the tremendous number of passages that fall to be considered, οἶκος renders *bayit* in the overwhelming majority of its occurrences (there are more than sixteen hundred of them, if I have counted correctly). The forty or so passages on which Stauffer builds his thesis of the 'ritual formula' can hardly be regarded as of major importance numerically in relation to that number. Yet only a complete assembly of the examples could yield an understanding of the true relationship and total picture of the data for comparison with that of the New Testament usage; and hence everything appears in a different perspective. Even if οἶκος in the sense of 'family' should occur in the Septuagint as a 'ritual formula', this usage is so relatively rare, the consequences drawn by Stauffer from it and the claim to their general validity cannot possibly be sustained by it. A similar judgment applies to the final conclusion that Stauffer deduces (from about seventeen places): 'In the concept *oikos*, the *oikos*-formula "he and his (whole) house", and the terms *panoikia* and *panoiki*, Greek Bible has in view not simply the children in addition to the adults, but the children *quite especially*, and not least any *little children* who might be present.'[1] In my opinion this apprehension must run quite differently when consideration is taken of the total phenomena; this stress on 'the children *quite especially*, and ... any *little children* who might be present'—the italics are Stauffer's—seems to me to be an exaggeration arising out of the heat of combat. But suppose we grant for a moment (what seems to me out of the question) that Stauffer's view is fully justified, including his presupposition that οἶκος in the Septuagint especially relates to the children, even including the little children; there would be no bridge from this position, or at best only a very narrow one, to the linguistic usage of the New Testament. For our investigation has shown that the relevant *oikos*-passages of the New Testament either permit no conclusion concerning the circle of persons in view, or they have in mind adults exclusively. And if anyone remains unconvinced by the foregoing considerations, being persuaded by the arguments of Jeremias and Stauffer for the view that the οἶκος passages of the New Testament (where οἶκος = family) emphasize the *children* who are presumed to be included therein, he must nevertheless not overlook the fact that what is given is a principle, not a practical answer. 'We do not know whether there were any little children belonging to the households of Stephanas, Lydia, or the keeper of the jail,' observes Stauffer rightly.[2] 'This does not mean to say that in every particular case in which the baptism of "a whole household" is mentioned, small children were actually present', explains

---

[1] p. 153.   [2] *Ibid.*

Jeremias.[1] One thing is at any rate indisputable: nowhere in connection with the οἶκος-passages in the New Testament is a child or an infant expressly named, let alone its baptism; and nowhere is any allusion made to any such baptism—a plain datum which we are in danger of forgetting when observing the confident assurance with which the existence of these children or infants is presupposed in the discussions about the 'oikos-formula'.

[1] p. 21.

9

The Blessing of the Children

ONE NEW TESTAMENT passage yet remains to be considered, namely the Gospel *pericope* that tells of the blessing of the children by Jesus, Mark 10.13 ff. and parallels. Jeremias devotes to it a detailed discussion,[1] contained within the two sides of a drawn bow provided by the beginning and end of his argument. At the beginning we read, 'The narrative itself, as we must emphasize, has nothing to do with baptism, but is "presacramental".'[2] In the closing paragraph it is nevertheless affirmed, 'If this conclusion is correct, the apostolic Church at some time between the years AD 60 and 70 advanced to the position where not alone the children of converts were baptized (a practice observed from the beginning) but also the children born in the community were baptized—and that as infants!'[3] The bridge by which Jeremias passed over from the position with which he began to that with which he concluded is furnished by Mark 10.13–16 and parallels. But can the bridge bear this burden of proof?

Jeremias gives the kernel of his position by printing in synoptic fashion the texts of Matt. 18.3, Mark 10.15 = Luke 18.17, John 3.5, Justin, *Apol.* I, 61.4 and *Const. Apost.* VI, 15.5. The diagram is intended to illustrate what deductions were drawn from the narrative of the blessing of the children by Jesus: 'Not only was the general summons inferred from it to lead the children to Jesus by precept and example, but also the command to give them to him through baptism.'[4] Now it is certainly true that this *pericope* must have been viewed as authorizing the baptism of children and/or infants by those who practised infant baptism. But infant baptism must have come on the scene first! Jeremias affirms (and this is the first step of his goal): 'The application of this passage about the blessing of the children to baptism was not first made at the end of the second century, but must be considerably older.'[5] He considers that John 3.5 depends on

[1] pp. 48–55. [2] p. 49.
[3] p. 68 of the German edition. The last paragraph of this discussion has been omitted from the English edition.
[4] p. 50. [5] *Ibid.*

Mark 10 and that this itself proves that Christians related the *pericope* to baptism; Justin is likewise held to be dependent on Mark 10 and not on John 3.5, as has hitherto wrongfully been assumed. By this means a bridge is constructed from the composition of Mark's Gospel over the end of the first century (John's Gospel) to the middle of the second century (Justin), and Jeremias is able to conclude, 'We see then that, as early as the end of the first century AD, Mark 10.15 = Luke 18.17 was applied to baptism.'[1] In addition to all this the usage of κωλύειν on the lips of Jesus is believed to provide an allusion that Mark 10 belongs to the context of baptism.[2]

Taking this last point first, there is no doubt, as O. Cullmann has shown,[3] that the verb κωλύειν is found as a technical term in connection with certain baptismal texts, cf. e.g. Acts 11.17 in Peter's report on the baptism in the house of Cornelius, etc. But there is no indication of such a context in Mark 10; a rejoinder is there made to disciples *hindering the approach* of the children to Jesus: ἄφετε τὰ παιδία ἔρχεσθαι πρός με, μὴ κωλύετε αὐτά, i.e. κωλύειν is employed with the meaning which has been customary from earliest times, namely to 'hinder'. *Perhaps* at a later time, when a developed baptismal liturgy had come into being with a question concerning hindrances to baptism, an echo of baptism was perceived also in the κωλύειν of Mark 10.14; such a possibility should not be excluded, but I do not believe that it can be postulated for this early time. κωλύειν appears twenty-three times in the New Testament and in only a very small percentage of cases can it be related to baptism, by far the preponderate number remain in the frame of the common linguistic usage. Only where baptism is expressly mentioned does an interpretation of κωλύειν as a *terminus technicus* for baptism seem possible to me.

With regard to the citation from Justin's *Apology*, I, 61.4, which occupies the fourth division of his synopsis, Jeremias has decidedly moderated the position which he maintained in the German edition.[4] He now writes:

---

[1] p. 53.   [2] pp. 53 f.

[3] *Baptism in the New Testament*, ET, 1950: Appendix, 'Traces of an Ancient Baptismal Formula in the New Testament', pp. 71 ff.

[4] In order to clarify the debate and the issues concerning this text, I reproduce what I wrote in the German edition of this book, p. 69. 'The passage from Justin is an important link in Jeremias' chain of evidence; he strongly opposes the view that it depends on John 3.5. Accordingly he writes . . . (There follows the quotation reproduced in the above paragraph but *without any reference to Justin's allusion to John 3.4.*) I cannot assent to his view—not because I have been convinced by the "introductory manuals", for the simple text of Justin is enough. The passage in I 61, cited by Jeremias, καὶ γὰρ ὁ Χριστὸς εἶπεν· "Ἂν μὴ ἀναγεννηθῆτε, οὐ μὴ εἰσέλθητε εἰς τὴν βασιλείαν τῶν οὐρανῶν, has an immediate continuation in I 61.5: "Ὅτι δὲ καὶ ἀδύνατον εἰς τὰς μήτρας τῶν τεκουσῶν τοὺς ἅπαξ γενομένους ἐμβῆναι, φανερὸν πᾶσίν ἐστι. This seems with transparent clarity to take up the question of Nicodemus in John 3.4, πῶς δύναται ἄνθρωπος γεννηθῆναι γέρων ὤν; μὴ δύναται εἰς τὴν κοιλίαν τῆς μητρὸς αὐτοῦ δεύτερον εἰσελθεῖν καὶ γεννηθῆναι; which itself was prompted by the statement of Jesus (John 3.3) to which John 3.5 forms a parallel, ἐὰν μή τις γεννηθῆναι ἐξ ὕδατος καὶ

'The fourth formulation of our saying (Justin, *Apol.* I, 61.4) is commonly reckoned a quotation from John 3.5, especially as Justin in the following sentence makes an allusion to John 3.4; accordingly our passage is regularly cited in introductory manuals to the New Testament as evidence that Justin used the Gospel of John, although there is nowhere in Justin a demonstrable word for word quotation from the Gospel of John. Even formulation IV is not in that category, but is instead a reproduction of Matt. 18.3, and is only influenced in the one word ἀναγεννηθῆτε by John 3.5 (γεννηθῇ ἄνωθεν).'[1] If Justin 'knew the Nicodemus story,' as Jeremias further states—and in view of *Apol.* I, 61.5 that is plainly not to be doubted—it seems to me that the position of Jeremias, already weakened in the English edition, is quite untenable. The decisive thing is not whether Justin follows the 'oral tradition' in his citation but whether he knows the Gospel of John.[2]

Further, the view of Jeremias that John 3.5 directly refers back to Mark 10.15 does not seem to me admissible. Mark speaks of receiving the kingdom of God 'as a child' (ὡς παιδίον) but John of being born of water and Spirit (3.5) or of being born from above (3.3). Jeremias regards these as equivalents: 'While the Synoptics (among whom Matthew's version is most sharply coloured by Semitic turns of phrase) speak of "becoming a child again" (Matthew) or "receiving the kingdom of God like a little child" (Mark, Matthew), John speaks of "being born again". The Synoptics thus lay more emphasis on the human attitude (ὡς παιδίον "by becoming like a child"), and John on the action of God. In essence, however, both say the same: a complete new beginning of life is the pre-condition of anyone finding admission under the rule of God.'[3] Here an identification is made of matters which, in my judgment we have as little right to identify as we have to equate the theology of the Gospel of John with that of the Synoptics. 'Being born again of water and Spirit' is not the same as 'becoming like a child' (Matt. 18.3) or 'receiving the kingdom of God like a child' (Mark 10.15); to turn back to the condition of a child is something quite different from that which the Gospel of John has in mind.[4] Undoubtedly Matt. 18.3 and Mark 10.15=Luke 18.17 belong to a single context, but there is no straight line from this context to John 3.5. Both sayings, despite their difference, have a common root in a dominical

πνεύματος, οὐ δύναται εἰσελθεῖν εἰς τὴν βασιλείαν τοῦ Θεοῦ. Justin, *Apol.* I, 61. *and* 45 appear to me to place beyond all dispute the conviction that Justin did indeed refer back to John's Gospel (and in my view also a tradition parallel to the Gospel, or otherwise connected with it) and at the same time to exclude Justin's dependence on Mark 10.'
[1] p. 52. [2] By Justin's time, of course, the Gospel of John had long been current.
[3] p. 52. [4] See below, pp. 104 f.

G

utterance; but that which has sprung independently from this root belongs to a different theological world. Moreover, John 3.5 stands in close connection with Justin and the parallels in Clement of Alexandria, etc. I am constrained to the view that the bridge erected by Jeremias does not sustain the burden of proof that he wants to place upon it, and indeed, if I may say so, the bridge does not exist at all. The Synoptics on the one hand and John and Justin on the other stand on two sides of a divide. The *Apostolic Constitutions*, although they are to be associated with the John and Justin group, belong to a much later time.

Again the external parallelism of the words is but apparent. The solemn beginning which they have in common (ἀμὴν λέγω ὑμῖν in Matt. 18.3, Mark 10.15 = Luke 18.17 and ἀμὴν ἀμὴν λέγω σοι in John 3.5) is far from having the significance that Jeremias attributes to it. Jeremias affirms: 'That in all five formulations we have to do with one and the same saying appears from the agreement in structure: a) in all four Gospels the logion is introduced by "Truly" (ἀμήν; John + ἀμήν) "I say unto you" (λέγω ὑμῖν; John, "thee", σοι).'[1] A glance in the concordance shows that Matthew has sayings of Jesus beginning with ἀμὴν λέγω ὑμῖν (σοι) thirty-one times, Mark fourteen times, and Luke seven times. John has the formula with his characteristic doubling of the ἀμήν twenty-five times. The external parallelism in the commencement of the sayings therefore does not suffice to prove their literary dependence on one another. The introductory formula occurs too frequently for that (only unusual agreements afford the *possibility* of affirming their literary dependence). Moreover the Fourth Evangelist has extended the use of the formula; like the other evangelists he has manifestly applied it in accordance with his own free judgment. The other agreement of structure postulated by Jeremias, 'b) in all the formulations a negative condition is added ("unless", ἐὰν μή),'[2] is to be found elsewhere and that similarly in connection with the solemn introductory formula; in addition to John 3.3 cf. also John 5.19, 'Amen, amen I tell you, the Son can do nothing by himself, except (ἂν μή, or ἐὰν μή as P66, Κ ADW. θpl.) what he the sees Father doing. . . .' The 'agreement of structure' therefore by no means justifies the view that in the passages under discussion we are dealing with 'one and the same saying' which has been taken over from one text to another; nor can the proof material that has been adduced carry the burden laid upon it. It is too insubstantial to justify the belief that from John 3.5 we can perceive 'with certainty' that 'the verse Mark 10.15 = Luke 18.17 was early interpreted as referring to baptism,'[3] a baptism, be it noted, which is applied to

---

[1] p. 51.   [2] *Ibid.*   [3] *Ibid.*

children or infants, concerning whom not a word occurs in John 3! That again is a point easily overlooked when one is reading the arguments of Jeremias, as also the fact that in John 3 a conversation with Nicodemus is reported, who was of an age such as one can but hope to attain!

10

When and Why was Infant Baptism
Introduced?

WE HAVE adjudged that it was not till after the Church had begun to baptize infants that she interpreted the *pericope* of the blessing of the children as authorizing her action. But when did she do that? We know that *c.* AD 200 there were circles in Carthage desiring infant baptism, and about 250 it was the rule demanded by the bishops in North Africa. About 230–250 Origen in Palestine characterized it as the 'custom of the Church' (*observantia ecclesiae*), and about 220 the *Church Order* of Hippolytus in Rome included little children in the baptismal order. This may be regarded as an assured result, apart from the *Church Order* of Hippolytus, which is subject to certain doubts regarding its section on infant baptism. Yet even in the third century infant baptism is plainly not the rule everywhere, for in those very areas where it had secured a firm place in the Church, the custom of baptizing children after attaining a maturer age remained in force alongside it, as the inscriptions testify. There were indeed some circles, it would seem, and even whole areas of the Church, in which continence in marriage was officially expected of Christians in full standing, hence the renunciation of children on their part; we must hear further about these, but for such people (theoretically at least) there could be no talk of baptizing either children or infants.[1] With this should be compared Marcion's demand of members of his counter-church, which was widespread in all the provinces of the Church from the second century on; in accordance with his foundational principles he made either celibacy or, for those already married, at least continence in the married state a requirement for full membership. Precisely the same thing happened among the Gnostics.

The custom that meets us in the fourth century of 'postponing' baptism, a usage observed in circles of deep spirituality, could certainly not

[1] Cf. the well-known essay by Karl Müller, *Die Forderung der Ehelosigkeit für alle Getauften in der alten Kirche*, Tübingen, 1927, published again in: *Aus der akademischen Arbeit, Vorträge und Aufsätze*, Tübingen, 1930, pp. 67–79.

have originated *ex nihilo*. It can be satisfactorily explained only when it is recognized that infant baptism was not an absolutely binding requirement everywhere in the Church, or at least that it was not compulsory in certain quarters, and that with that practice existed a baptism of children of a mature age which met with no ecclesiastical objection. The complete unaffectedness with which Gregory Nazianzus, at that time patriarch of the capital of the empire (!), recommended the baptism of children at the age of three years[1] cannot be accidental. It cannot have been due to his arbitrariness or personal whim; in this respect Gregory must have been conscious of remaining within the limits of what was possible and usual in the Church. From this point of view the arguments of Jeremias concerning the 'great crisis in infant baptism'[2] that took place in the fourth century are in need of correction. Not only Gregory Nazianzus[3] but also Basil the Great, both highly esteemed bishops and theologians, can call for the early baptism of children with complete lack of prejudice, while at the same time they represent in their own persons examples of a very far-reaching 'postponement of baptism', to use terms of Jeremias. In reality this 'postponement of baptism' in the fourth century represents the last epoch of the practice of the ancient Church; it is not something new and unheard of, as Jeremias would have us believe.[4] The only new thing about it is the scrupulousness observed in the Emperor Constantine and others, who waited for baptism till such time as it seemed to them to guarantee their salvation with certainty. This epoch manifestly came to an end in the fourth century—at least in the West. In Augustine's time infant baptism is an established custom; he is able to use it in his controversy with Pelagianism as a powerful argument for his teaching on the original depravity of the newly-born. The Pelagians also have to bear infant baptism as an institution, even though it does not fit their views, so firmly is it anchored in the regulations and the consciousness of the Church.

It can be no accident, as has been emphasized already, that all our information about the existence of infant baptism comes from the period between AD 200 and 250. At that time we hear of its observance in Africa, Palestine and Italy; in each case the way in which it is spoken of conveys the impression that the practice takes its rise at the end of the second century. For the time before this we do not possess a single piece of information that gives concrete testimony to the existence of infant baptism.

---

[1] On this cf. p. 46.   [2] pp. 87 ff.   [3] On this see p. 41 n. 4.
[4] Jeremias speaks about the 'singular behaviour of the theologians'. 'They are silent. Not that they opposed the practice of infant baptism—of that we have not the slightest evidence. But no one has a clear policy in face of the crisis' (p. 91). Is that not of itself a hint that the situation must have been other than it appears to Jeremias?

Jeremias himself will have to admit that, since all his proofs are and remain *circumstantial proofs*, whatever may be thought of their soundness. Even the individual who still inclines to regard them as satisfactory will not be able to contest it. To this day nobody can prove an actual case of the baptism of an infant in the period before AD 200 on the basis of 'the sources, which begin to be more abundant at this time', to use Jeremias' words.[1] That our entire sources, at least when allowed their literal sense, have in view only the baptism of adults, or at best the baptism of older children, can as little be contested.

But how is the change to infant baptism to be explained? When and in what manner was it accomplished? Our investigation would be incomplete if it did not attempt to give an answer to this question, for only a positive answer can complete the circle. It is by no means a simple matter, for even when exercising the utmost diligence of research into the early period of the Church, an investigation into the development of baptism can much more easily establish what did not exist, according to our sources, than to make positive assertions as to the actual course of development. Contrary to Jeremias, I am inclined to think that our sources must 'flow' much more richly, not only up to the year 200 but also on to Constantine and after, in order to make unexceptionable statements possible. It is true, if I may put it figuratively, that the number of lights multiplies in the course of the development, and they serve to illuminate the obscurity of the past. But there still remain shadowy areas, concerning which we can but assume that the same holds good of them as of the sections illuminated by the teachings or our sources. On the other hand, it is obvious that we can only operate with the sections that are actually known to us.

On that basis the course of events may be outlined somewhat as follows. First, the development leading to infant baptism was determined by external factors. Up to the end of the second century Christianity must be seen as a small minority in the Roman empire.[2] Admittedly this fellowship had grown many times its original size since its early days. But this growth quite definitely had come about from *without*, through the entry of new converts, who most commonly were adults. It was only after the Church had attained a certain strength that the 'inner' growth, i.e. the increase in the number of Christians through children born among them, began numerically to play a significant role. Naturally there were births in Chris-

---

[1] p. 57. His language in fact is a little stronger:' . . . the sources *which are already flowing richly in this time*', p. 58 of the German edition.

[2] Cf. Harnack's *Mission und Ausbreitung des Christentums in den ersten drei Jahrhunderten*[4], 1924, especially II, p. 529, the evidence of the texts and estimate of their contribution.

tian marriages at all times (and despite the restrictive regulations of the Syrian Church, in all areas of the Church also). And undoubtedly the growth was the same in percentage at all times, apart from the fact that it was precisely the second century, with its development of the Marcionite counter-church and Gnosticism at the expense of the great Church, that saw a considerable diminution of the number of births among Christians, even when reckoned on a percentage basis.[1] But these numbers sink into the background in face of the stream of converts from without. Harnack regards the time of Commodus and of his successors (i.e. the period after AD 180) as the time when the first great forward thrust of the Christian Church took place. In truth the statements of Tertullian (and indirectly those also of Origen) lead to the conclusion that the number of Christians and of the Church in the Roman Empire c. AD 200 was very considerable. With the increasing strength of the Church the absolute number of the children born in it also greatly increased, and their 'belonging' to the Church, i.e. their baptism, becomes an ever greater problem. This problem may well have been rendered more acute by the complete separation of the Marcionites and the Gnostics, or at least the end of sympathy with them; it caused the percentage and also the absolute number of births among the 'old members' of the Church quite suddenly to increase.

But this explanation for the emergence of infant baptism c. AD 200 remains external, and by itself it is insufficient. An *inner* motive must be added. If we consider Cyprian and Origen we find two statements which, in the last resort, are fully harmonious. Cyprian declares that a new-born child 'has not sinned, except that, being born after the flesh according to Adam, he has contracted the contagion of the ancient death at its earliest birth; yet on this very account he approaches the more easily to the reception of the forgiveness of sins, because it is not his own sins that are forgiven him but the sins of another.'[2] Although the child is without sin of its own, it is nevertheless ensnared in the sinfulness of mankind from Adam and therefore needs the cleansing in baptism of this 'sin of another' (*aliena peccata*), since no one ought to be hindered from receiving grace. The statements of Origen are quite parallel: to objections against infant baptism he counters ever and again the view that the saying of Scripture (Job 14.4 f. etc.) applies even to the newborn, 'No one is pure from stain, yea though he be but one day old.'[3] From the first day of his life an infant

---

[1] Cf. the essay of K. Müller.
[2] '. . . *nihil peccavit, nisi quod secundum Adam carnaliter natus contagium mortis antique prima nativitate contraxit, qui ad remissam peccatorum accipiendam hoc ipso facilius accedit quod illi remittuntur non propria sed aliena peccata*', Ep 64.5, CSEL 3.2, pp. 720 f., Kraft no. 19a. [3] *Nemo mundus a sorde, nec si unius diei sit vita eius.* For references see p. 47 n. 1.

participates in sin. Admittedly a child just born cannot itself commit sin: *et tamen habet peccatum*! If we compare these consentient statements with the view of Tertullian concerning the 'innocent age' of children who do not need to 'hasten to the remission of sins' (*De bapt.* 18.5), we face a complete opposition of views; and from this opposition a different attitude to infant baptism of necessity arises. So long as it is believed that children are without sin, infant baptism is not needed. For baptism is a bath of cleansing, in which a man is washed clean from his sins.[1] If a child born of Christian parents is sinless, it does not need this bath of cleansing. As soon as the conviction becomes prevalent, however, that an infant participates in sin, even when born of Christian parents, infant baptism as a requirement or practice is unavoidable. In the age of Tertullian, towards the close of the second century, this view has manifestly become widespread, or at least has begun to win its way. The utterances of Tertullian himself show its development, and Irenaeus appears to incline to such an interpretation. Accordingly we find the beginnings of infant baptism in this period.

Tertullian is certainly not the last to subscribe to this view of the purity of the new-born child; note e.g. the complaint of the Carthaginian Synod of 411 against the teaching of Pelagius, who maintained that infants are in that state in which Adam was before he sinned.[2] But neither was he the first. Rather, I would say that this estimate of the age of infancy can be demonstrated to go back to the beginnings of the Church. Occasionally expression is given to it.[3] To this context belongs the view of Paul, represented in I Cor. 7.14, that the children of mixed marriages (and correspondingly of Christian marriages) are ἅγια.[4] The same applies, possibly not in intention but certainly in effect, to the words of our Lord handed on in the Synoptic tradition about the children; I especially have in mind the affirmation that a man must become like a child if he would enter the kingdom of God, and the saying that the kingdom of God must be received as a child (in the *pericope* about the blessing of the children, dealt with above). Contrary to Jeremias, I would maintain that the early Church interpreted these words as implying the immediacy of little children to God, not their baptism—till a different explanation prevailed on

---

[1] This is common to all statements about baptism and is so obvious, it is unnecessary to prove it with the aid of lists of quotations and sources. Naturally the theological understanding of Christian baptism goes beyond this assertion, nevertheless in its basic significance baptism remains a bath of cleansing.

[2] *Quod infantes qui nascuntur, in eo statu sint, in quo fuit Adam ante transgressionem.* On this see Loofs, *Dogmengeschichte*[6], 1959, p. 340.

[3] Cf. p. 56, etc.

[4] I Cor. 14.20 may be adduced as a parallel; I Peter 2.2 may also be compared.

the basis of changed presuppositions. Such an understanding provides the background for the statements of Paul, even if perchance the influence of ideas current in the world about him also played a part.[1] For Paul the child born in a non-Christian marriage is ἀκάθαρτος, i.e. unclean in the cultic sense. It is characteristic that the term becomes modified in its significance, and in Christian terminology as early as the Apostolic Fathers it is transferred to moral dispositions (a usage which may even be found in the New Testament).[2]

In the Apostolic Fathers we repeatedly find the presumption of the 'innocence' (in the original meaning of the term) of children unambiguously intimated. In the *Letter of Barnabas* 6.11 it is declared that Christ renews Christians in the remission of sins as if they were born for a second time, 'so that they should have the soul of children' (ὡς παιδίων ἔχειν τὴν ψυχήν). In the *Shepherd of Hermas*, right at the beginning of the second Mandate, and so in a prominent position, it is written: 'Keep simplicity and be guileless, and thou shalt be as little children, who do not know the wickedness that destroys the life of men.'[3] The whole of chapter 29 of the ninth Parable is concerned with this theme. Here the twelfth mountain of Sim. IX, 1 is interpreted; it is completely white, and in the series of the twelve mountains that symbolize the Church it represents the summit of possibility. The believers who belong to this group are 'very babes, into whose heart no guile enters, neither have they learned what wickedness is, but they have remained as babes for ever'.[4] Since they have not violated the commands of God in any respect, but have passed their whole life in this childlike purity, they receive immediately a place in the kingdom of God.[5] Accordingly an exhortation is given to Hermas and to all Christians to remain and to become as βρέφη, without guile (κακίαν μὴ ἔχοντες).[6] Shortly afterwards this exhortation recurs. The angel of repentance pronounces a blessing on all who are 'guileless as infants'.[7] Among the Apologists we have already discussed the statement of Aristides (15.11) that Christians give God abounding thanks (ὑπερευχαριστοῦσιν) at the death of a child (νήπιον) because it has died sinless.[8] It was plain to us that the view of Jeremias, that this text 'can hardly refer to the innocence of childhood, but more probably to the forgiveness which is given in bap-

---

[1] Cf. above pp. 83 f. [2] Cf. Arndt and Gingrich under ἀκάθαρτος.

[3] Ἁπλώτατα ἔχε καὶ ἄκακος γίνου καὶ ἔσῃ ὡς τὰ νήπια τὰ μὴ γινώσκοντα τὴν πονηρίαν τὴν ἀπολλύουσαν τὴν ζωὴν τῶν ἀνθρώπων, Mand. II, 1.

[4] . . . . νήπια βρέφη . . ., οἷς οὐδεμία κακία ἀναβαίνει ἐπὶ τὴν καρδίαν οὐδὲ ⟨ἔγνω⟩σαν, τί ἐστι πονηρία, ἀλλὰ πάντοτε ἐν νηπιότητι διέμειναν, Sim. IX, 29.1.

[5] Sim. IX, 29.2. [6] Sim. IX, 29.3.

[7] *Felices . . . quicumque estis innocentes sicut infantes*, Sim. IX, 31.3.

[8] See above, p. 56.

tism',[1] is artificial. Its incorrectness is demonstrable. Athenagoras in his *De resurrectione mortuorum* 14 says of very little children that they will not be judged at the resurrection.[2] Here also the very young child is regarded as sinless, free from any taint arising before or after birth that may be traceable to the sin of Adam.

This collection of evidence could undoubtedly be increased, but its present extent is sufficient to demonstrate that the belief in the sinlessness of infants was held continuously till the time of Tertullian (Athenagoras brings us to about AD 180). So long as and wherever this assumption held good, infant baptism was plainly not necessary, indeed it was superfluous, the more so while the eschatological expectation of the nearness of the End persisted, and it certainly did continue right into the heart of the second century.[3] If the last day is to come at any moment, it will take the sinless infants and little children immediately to God. Towards the end of the second century Montanism destroyed what remained of this 'near expectation', while the *Shepherd of Hermas* produced an argument that theologically explained and justified the postponement of the Second Advent. From the moment that the taint of original sin was believed to apply to the newborn child, its baptism became a necessity under the new presuppositions, for it could no longer be assumed that the Last Day would come in the lifetime of these children. So far as we are able to judge from the sources, this fundamental change was completed about AD 200 or shortly before; i.e. it followed not long after the change in the eschatological outlook. Accordingly from that time the custom of infant baptism spread, and in Africa apparently with considerable force.

A hint may be found in Tertullian how the baptism of children was actually regarded. He does not desire to keep children back from baptism absolutely; they should come to it when they have grown somewhat: 'Let them come when they grow older; let them come when they are able to learn, when they can be instructed whither they should come; let them become Christians when they can know Christ.'[4] Obviously that corresponds not only to what he believes to be right but to the practice of the Church hitherto. Tertullian moreover is not of the opinion that children remain in the '*innocens aetas*'[5] indefinitely. Even with children born of Christian parents the 'innocence' is lost later; Tertullian actually gives the point of time when that takes place: it happens in puberty.[6] A child born of a pagan marriage, is in the greatest danger from birth onwards by

---

[1] p. 71.   [2] Schwartz, TU IV, 2, 64.
[3] Only under this presupposition is a phenomenon like Montanism to be explained.
[4] *De baptismo* 18.5, cf. above, pp. 61 ff.   [5] *Ibid.*   [6] *De anima* 38.1.

reason of heathen superstitions. On these grounds baptism is a requisite both for children born of pagan marriages and for those who come from Christian parents so soon as the presuppositions are fulfilled ('when they have become able to know Christ', etc.). To these statements of Tertullian we should add that of the *Apology* of Aristides, 15.6,[1] which takes us into the first decades of the second century, and here we are confronted with a parallel utterance: the children of Christian families are 'instructed, that they become Christians'. This happens out of love for them, for they also should become partakers of the blessings of Christ's people. 'And when they have become Christians [through baptism], they call them "brethren" without distinction.' Here we have the same view as in Tertullian but seventy or eighty years earlier. We are also given a picture as to how the practice of the churches prior to the close of the second century AD appeared: instruction was given and baptism administered to children when they had attained knowledge, at an age that required cleansing through the awakening of sin and destruction of original purity. This optimistic view at length becomes lost; it gives way to a realistic conception of the corruption that dwells even in infancy on account of the sinfulness of mankind since Adam. With an outlook of this kind, the foundation of the earlier practice disappears. But it does not cease suddenly; it lasts on in considerable areas of the Church, conformably with the perpetuation of the notion of the innocence and purity of children. That this latter conviction endured beyond the age of Tertullian is hinted at pretty plainly by the Pelagians. Their opposition to the idea of original sin implanted in the newborn child from Adam had from the first the widest sympathies in the theology and church of the East; it also found a considerable echo in the West, precisely because their view corresponded to a widespread attitude. But by that time infant baptism had everywhere penetrated so universally and so fundamentally, it could provide Augustine with the decisive argument for the refutation of Pelagianism: If children have no sin when they are born, why are they baptized? Here the original position has been reversed—the guns have been turned round!

If an illustration is needed of the continuing dissemination and the abiding strength of the conception of the sinlessness of infants and children we have but to cast a glance at the Christian inscriptions. They can hardly be characterized as 'Pelagian' in the strict sense, yet it is astonishing how often the attribute *innocens, innocentissimus*, etc. occurs as a single predicate in the burial inscriptions of children. In so far as these concern neophytes[2]

---

[1] On this cf. above, p. 56.
[2] See e.g. Diehl I, 1485, 1485A, 1585C, 1491, 1497, 1507, etc.

they must obviously be understood in relation to baptismal purity. But such inscriptions are in the minority. By far the majority contain no explicit mention of this presupposition. In them we find *parvulus innocens*,[1] *iube(n)i innocentiss(imo)*,[2] *infanti innocentissime*,[3] *animae innocentissime*,[4] etc., etc. Long lists of this kind could be compiled, but they do not help us further; for apart from the difficulty of dating these inscriptions, we occasionally find in them a tendency to attribute the 'innocence' also to more advanced ages.[5] And even were it not so, it is yet possible that in them we have before us documents of a naïve attitude which glorifies the innocence of childhood in a romantic fashion; the last rays of that viewpoint shine on in our own day. In any case it is understandable from all this that what Jeremias calls the postponement of baptism is still to be found in the fourth century to a greater extent.

We have frequently pointed out that the terminology introduced by Jeremias into the discussion on infant- and child-baptism, as also the categories of thought that lie behind it, do not do justice to the actual situation of the early Church. The application of this judgment to the idea of 'missionary-baptism' has already been shown.[6] The same thing obtains regarding Jeremias' assertions on the 'postponement of baptism' and 'forbearing to baptize'. Jeremias holds that this phenomenon first occurs in the fourth century; indeed he is even able to give a precise date for it and to set it in its historical context. He writes, 'The dating of the crisis, which we have established, is instructive for the understanding of it. We have seen that the first demonstrable instance of Christian parents postponing the baptism of their children was in the year 329/30 . . . and that the ecclesiastical reaction against the postponement of baptism began about 365. The acute crisis, therefore, lies in the decades following the recognition of Christianity as the religion of the state, i.e. in that period during which countless numbers of pagans were flocking into the Church. It is no surprise to find that the superstitious conception of baptism which many of these pagans brought with them also had an influence upon Christian circles.'[7] This sounds convincing, but the facts speak another language. One needs only to remember the inscriptions of the third century, which exhibit this 'postponement of baptism' time and again; and these relate not only to catechumens and pagan families entering the Christian Church, as Jeremias has maintained, but also to Christian families. The 'crisis' of

---

[1] Diehl II, 3980 (Italy, undated).   [2] *Ibid.*, 3980A (Italy, undated).
[3] *Ibid.*, 2697 (Rome, undated; the child is two years two months old).
[4] *Ibid.*, 4018C (Rome, undated; the child is two years old).
[5] Cf. e.g. II, 2599, erected to the *innocentissimo fratre*, who is over thirty-three years old!   [6] Cf. above, pp. 42 ff.   [7] p. 95 .

which Jeremias speaks never existed, at least not in the manner he describes. The 'postponement of baptism' in that period is at all explicable only if it has had an earlier history, at least during the third century. That it occurs so often in the fourth century may *perhaps* have had specific causes, but to a large extent it is explained by the fact that a considerable change in the situation of the Church occurred in the fourth century and our information in all areas of the Church's life increases in a manifold way, so that things emerge into the clear light of day which formerly lay in obscurity, although they existed earlier in exactly the same form.

Jeremias further explains: 'We hear in the history of the early Church nothing about two kinds of Christians, baptized and unbaptized; had baptism been withheld from children born to Christian parents, then there would very soon have grown up a mixed crowd of baptized and unbaptized Christians living alongside each other'.[1] That is not quite right, at least it is seen amiss. Probably the Christian faith began with a 'mixed crowd of baptized and unbaptized Christians living alongside of each other'. For we hear nothing—or as good as nothing[2]—concerning the practice of baptism among the communities gathered in the period between John's baptism of repentance and Pentecost, and in any case the 'baptized' had only received the baptism of John. Jeremias' argumentation is determined by modern ideas. Where (according to Paul's view) a Christian spouse sanctifies the pagan, and where the child of such a marriage is *per se* 'holy', whether it has been baptized or not, ideas such as those reflected in the expositions of Jeremias have no place. The commingling of baptized and unbaptized members of the community was no problem in that era. Jeremias' 'mixed crowd of baptized and unbaptized Christians' did exist in an organizational form from the time when a man who made known his desire to become a Christian was not immediately received into the Church through baptism but had to submit to a period of instruction and probation, i.e. from the time when the catechumenate began to develop; but nobody thought anything of it, for this juxtaposition belonged to the very existence of the Church. The children, who to this point were not baptized, fitted in easily enough: depending on the time in which we find ourselves and the position adopted by a church (which was not the same at all times and in all places),[3] they were reckoned either with the full

---

[1] p. 57.   [2] Cf. below, p. 114.

[3] We have no right to assume, as unfortunately so often happens in investigations into Church history, that the Church in all its provinces, or even all the churches of a single province, always exhibited the same position in teaching and practice in the earliest years. That is an impermissible projection of later conditions into early times. Take only the example of the parousia expectation: if in many places in the first half of the second century it was still a living hope and comparable to the glow of the primitive era, else-

members or with the 'catechumens'. The boundaries fluctuate; from the moment that children as well as others received instruction in preparation for cleansing by baptism of the ἀκαθαρσία (in its new sense) they had acquired through life thus far, they practically belonged to the category of 'catechumens'. They became full Christians only through baptism and participation in the eucharist.

The two other *argumenta e silentio* brought forward by Jeremias[1] also do not correspond to historical reality, or they spring from an inadequate view of the history. What does the assertion, 'Nowhere does the custom appear as the special doctrine of a party or sect,'[2] signify for the existence or non-existence of infant baptism in the early years of the Church? That we have in infant baptism 'one of the few Church usages in relation to which the great Church everywhere was completely unanimous'[3] is an assertion to be proved, not an argument with which anything can be proved. The early Church in both East and West attributed to the 'apostolic tradition' many things that actually arose in a later time, as is well known to every investigator of early Church history. This however is but peripheral. More important are two other arguments used by Jeremias. He affirms: 'We have no information about the introduction of a practice deviating from previous custom. In particular nowhere in the literature of the ancient Church do we find discussion on the question whether children of Christian parents should be baptized. Had the custom of baptizing them not been introduced until the second century, it would have been quite inconceivable that the introduction of so startling a novelty would have left no trace in the sources, which begin to be more abundant at this time.'[4] In view of Tertullian's volume *De baptismo*, it cannot well be maintained that the transition to infant baptism has 'left no trace in the sources'. Here is to be found with all desirable audibility the echo of the new usage and the protest against it. It is also clear from Origen that an opposition to the practice of infant baptism existed—at least it seems plain enough to me! Moreover this baptism of infants was not introduced overnight but came about gradually—in harmony with a changing consciousness both among the theologians and in the Church. For a long time infant baptism in a whole number of areas existed alongside the previously established custom of baptizing children at a later age and did not take its place with a claim to exclusiveness.

Finally Jeremias states: 'The fact that no special rite for child baptism

where at the same time it could also be in process of disappearing or of being considerably reduced. The same thing applies in other respects.
[1] Cf. the summary given above, pp. 36 f.   [2] p. 57.   [3] *Ibid.*   [4] *Ibid.*

was introduced speaks also for the early practice of baptizing Christian children. Had the practice not been introduced until a time when the baptismal ritual had reached a rather fuller state of development, the Church would surely not have been content simply to apply the ritual of adult baptism to children.'[1] This argument not only permits of a satisfactory solution, it can actually be turned against its advocate. It is true that the ritual of adult baptism was transferred to infants, although from the beginning it necessitated the assistance of a 'sponsor' (*pater*), who answered and spoke up for the infant during the baptism (cf. the *Church Order* of Hippolytus). But why was this necessary? Without doubt because to this time it was the custom for children to be baptized at an age when they could themselves assume these functions. When they had passed through the Christian instruction and already reached a certain age (Tertullian puts it at the age of puberty), the formulary for adult baptism fitted them without any difficulty. When the practice of baptizing children immediately after birth was begun, the formula that had hitherto been used for older children was *further* applied. A firm tradition had already grown up in connection with the baptism of children; it was too firm for people to wish to change it, or even for them to be able to do so, especially since children of more advanced years continued to be baptized and the formula in any case remained in use.

p. 57.

I I

Postscript: Infant Baptism Today?

AN EXAMINATION of the beginnings of infant baptism at the end of the second century not only yields a self-consistent picture which does justice to the extant sources, it also creates the impression that a consistent picture can be arrived at only through a like historical approach. We now have to ask the question, What does this mean for the practice of infant baptism today? We step beyond the bounds of our theme in raising it, but at least the attempt should be made to offer a few words on this burning issue.

In the modern discussion we are continually meeting an attitude which is determined by the following patterns of thought:

A. Practice of infant baptism in the age of the New Testament and in the ancient Church. } = Necessity of the practice of infant baptism today.

or

B. No practice of infant baptism in the age of the New Testament and the ancient Church. } = Necessity of the practice of adult baptism today.

Scheme B appears to me to involve a short circuit of thinking at the decisive point—at any rate on the assumption that in the New Testament baptism is understood in a causative sense[1] and not simply as cognitive.

O. Cullmann has rightly and emphatically maintained that no proof from Scripture can be adduced to support the conclusion that follows on Scheme B.[2] Tertullian long ago aptly said of the attitude manifest in B: 'In insisting on the warrant of Scripture for a different side from their own, men take it for granted that the support of Scripture should no less appear

---

[1] In my judgment this view alone corresponds to the findings of New Testament research, but it cannot be expounded here in detail; see the relevant literature.

[2] *Baptism in the New Testament*, ET, 1950, p. 26: 'Those who dispute the Biblical character of infant baptism have to reckon with the fact that adult baptism for sons and daughters born of Christian parents, which they recommend, is even worse attested by the New Testament than infant baptism (for which certain possible traces are discoverable) and indeed lacks any kind of proof.'

on their side.'[1] And this proof from Scripture (on the basis, I repeat, of the causative interpretation) cannot be produced.

Indeed, we must go further: The New Testament undoubtedly makes statements about the character and significance of baptism for the Christian, but it makes these statements without providing any binding prescription as to the manner in which it is to be carried out,[2] and in particular without any clearly binding directions concerning the *time* of its administration. In the Acts of the Apostles, and occasionally elsewhere, we are able to glimpse a few aspects of early Christian usage. From them we must conclude that infant baptism was not practised at that time, since these infants were regarded as ἅγια. The ancient Church perpetuates this tradition and only at the end of the second century departed from it, and that on theological grounds: so long as the Church assumed that children born of Christian parents were sinless, it abstained from infant baptism; so soon as it recognized the falsity of this presupposition, it began to ask for and introduce infant baptism. If belief in the sinful corruption of children from their birth is admitted by us—and to establish that is surely superfluous—then the necessity of infant baptism follows on it; this is in direct agreement with the ancient Church and accords with a profounder understanding of the teaching of the New Testament. Here the argument of Cyprian is still valid: 'The mercy and grace of God is not to be refused to any human being. For as the Lord says in his Gospel, "The Son of Man did not come to destroy man's lives but to save them"; as far as we can we must strive that, if possible, no soul be lost.'[3]

Hence in my view a third pattern emerges:

C. No (or no demonstrable) practice of infant baptism in the age of the New Testament and in the ancient Church till shortly before 200. } = Practice of infant baptism today.

This formula sounds paradoxical, but it is only apparently so. For the practice of infant baptism today can claim that it fulfils in a new time and

---

[1] *Expostulantes enim scripturae patrocinium in parte diuersa praeiudicant suae quoque parti scripturae patrocinium adesse debere, De Corona,* 11.4 (CC 2, p. 1042).

[2] To say that baptism must take place 'in the name of Christ' belongs to the presupposition of Christian baptism and is not to be classed with directions as to the nature and manner of its administration. Prescriptions of the latter order (baptism in running water, or in another kind if that is not available; the use of cold water, otherwise of warm; immersion, otherwise threefold pouring; previous fasting of the baptizer and of the baptizand, etc.) are first found in the *Didache* (chap. 7).

[3] *Nulli hominum nato misericordiam Dei et gratiam denegandam. nam cum Dominus in evangelio suo dicat: filius hominis non venit animas hominum perdere sed salvare, quantum in nobis est, si fieri potest, nulla anima perdenda est, Ep.* 64.2, CSEL 3, 2, p. 718.

H

in a new way what took place in early times in a different manner. Consider as another example of this the Lord's Supper: whatever the mode of our celebrating it today, and whatever our view of its institution, it requires no demonstration that we do not celebrate it in the manner of the New Testament age (we need only recall the 'Agape' of the Pauline communities). Nevertheless the Church claims, and surely with right, that what she does in a new time and in a new way is a legitimate performance of what took place in early times in another way. And many other instances could be cited. So far as baptism is concerned, we may recollect that in the time of Jesus baptism probably was either not practised at all or was exceptional.[1] Whoever followed the call of Jesus and submitted to his message was a disciple. Those who had received the baptism of John earlier belonged no less to the disciple group, but quite as many, if not the majority of people who followed the call of Jesus, did not submit to John's baptism. Should we draw the conclusion from this that baptism as such ought to be repudiated today? No, for it is quite impossible to bracket together our age and that of the New Testament, but it is possible for us to keep on making renewed efforts to realize the demands of the New Testament. According to the presuppositions that we share, the practice of infant baptism today belongs to that category.

By these 'presuppositions' I do not mean practical ecclesiastical necessities, such as that of maintaining the national Church, and other similar considerations which are often brought into the debate, but solely theological necessities. It is true that Luther's writings over the years about infant baptism differ greatly in theological importance, and much of what he wrote is deficient and open to criticism.[2] His work *To two Clergymen about Rebaptism*, is not free from this kind of thing. Nevertheless in this volume Luther, 'in brevity and in haste,'[3] said a good many things that in my estimation are of importance for our theme. Allow me to cite some of his words:

'In the third place, as I have observed, they take their stand on this saying: "He who believes and is baptized shall be saved." They wish to infer from this that no man should be baptized until he believes. On the contrary I say that they venture upon great presumptuousness. For if they intend to follow out this notion they must not baptize until they know of a

---

[1] Compare by way of example Stauffer's article quoted on p. 29. No other conclusion is possible from the utterances of the Gospels. The statement of John 4.1–2, which in any case is contradictory, cannot outweigh the absolute silence of the Synoptic Gospels concerning the practice of baptism through Jesus or the apostles.

[2] In so far as the relevant literature is inclined to make a hero of Luther it has difficulty in fitting large numbers of his utterances into the framework of infallibility constructed for them.   [3] WA 26, 173, 13.

surety that the candidate for baptism does believe. But how and when can they ever know that? have they become gods, so that they can see into the heart of the people and know whether they believe or not?'[1]

'You say, "He confesses that he has faith," etc. No, rather, keep confession out of it. The text does not say, "He who confesses", but "He who believes". His confession you have, certainly, but his faith you do not know; hence on your view you cannot satisfy this saying unless you also know his faith, because all men are liars and only God knows the heart. Whoever therefore will base baptism on the faith of the man seeking baptism must never baptize anyone, for even if you were to baptize a man a hundred times a day you cannot once know whether he believes.'[2]

'It is true that a man should believe for baptism, but baptism should not be administered on the basis of faith. It is one thing to have faith and another to trust in faith and so be baptized on the ground of faith. He who gets baptized on the basis of faith is not only uncertain, but is also an idolatrous denier of Christ; for he trusts and builds on something of his own, namely on a gift that God has given him, and not on God's word alone, precisely as another builds and reposes trust on his strength, his riches, power, wisdom, holiness, which are also gifts given by God.'[3]

This last word seems to me to touch on something decisive. The baptism of a child at a later age, on the ground that now, of his own decision, he fulfils the presupposition of Mark 16.16, 'He who believes and is baptized will be saved,' carries with it the danger of perverting baptism. Faith is made a presupposition for baptism which a man brings with him—it is made into a work that he does. Thereby not only is baptism destroyed from within, but also the entire insight of the Reformation:

'It is a work of the devil with him, when he admits faith but means a work and under the name and appearance of faith leads the poor people to trust in a work.'[4] 'For that is a real master-stroke of the devil, in urging Christians to forsake the righteousness of faith for the righteousness of works.'[5]

I do not get baptized, explains Luther, because I am sure of faith, but because God has commanded it and will have it. 'For even though I were never more sure of faith, yet am I sure of the command, since God enjoins baptism, sending forth the command for the whole world. Here I can make no mistake, for God's command cannot deceive; but he has never said or demanded or ordered anything about my faith.'[6] If God makes his

---

[1] WA 26, 154, 1–8.
[2] WA 26, 154, 16–25.
[3] WA 26, 164, 39–165, 7.
[4] WA 26, 161, 35–37.
[5] WA 26, 162, 17–18.
[6] WA 26, 164, 33–38

covenant with the world, 'who then can exclude the little children?'[1] 'Since he commands, all the world should receive it. On the basis of such a command (because nobody is excluded) we safely and freely baptize everybody, and nobody is excluded, unless he resists it and does not wish to receive such a covenant. When we baptize everyone according to his command, we leave to him the problem of how the baptizand believes; we have done enough when we preach and baptize. If we possess no special sayings that tell us to baptize the children, no more have we sayings that command us to baptize older people (i.e. adults). But since we have a command to offer everyone the universal gospel and the universal baptism, the children must also be included. We plant and water and leave God to give the increase.'[2]

[1] WA 26, 169, 21 f.   [2] WA 26, 169, 26–35.

INDEX OF BIBLICAL REFERENCES

OLD TESTAMENT

NEW TESTAMENT

INDEX OF SOURCES

INDEX OF MODERN AUTHORS

DATE